TEACH YOURSELF TO DRIVE IN 20 LESSONS

The Comprehensive Learner Drivers' Guide
- from Car Control to Driving Test

Mark Johnston

Spectrum Driving School Publishing

***

This book is partly a compilation, with parts taken from two of the author's other titles:

The twenty lessons in this book can be found in: 'Teach Your Kids to Drive in 20 Lessons: Supervising a Learner Driver - from Car Control to Driving Test'

This book also contains an edited version of: 'Hill Starts in Hillhead to Parking in Park Royal: The Learner Drivers' Guide to Passing the Driving Test'

***

CONTENTS

INTRODUCTION

Welcome to the easiest way for you to learn how to drive and to prepare for your driving test. This book will take you smoothly from that first Sunday-morning drive around a deserted car park, all the way through to your driving test, covering all aspects of car control and road knowledge, and giving you all the test information and manoeuvring skills you'll need.

The idea is to read one or all of the lessons here before heading out to your car to practise. Then revise the lessons just as often as you wish. Or, if you're about to start on a course of driving lessons, using this book as a firm foundation of knowledge, to set you on the right track.

These lessons have developed over my thirty year career as a driving instructor, teaching fifteen-hundred pupils and covering half-a-million driving instruction miles. My road experience also includes working as a lorry driver, as well as decades of motorcycling – and both trucks and bikes have taken me all over the UK and Europe. I've also written extensively on the subject of driving, both online and for publication.

The lessons here, then, are a result of a lifetime's road experience.

But what these lessons *aren't* is a rehash of any official-sounding government driving book. So, errors and omissions, though hopefully few, are nonetheless accepted! But, if you're able to practise the lessons, and develop as a driver, this is where the knowledge and experience of your **Supervisor** comes into the mix. We're all working together. I lay the foundations, you guys build on them.

Ah, yes…your Supervisor. That's what we'll call the person who's helping you with the practical aspects of your driving. This could be a professional driving instructor, or could just as easily be a friend or family member, but someone giving you their time – and quite possibly lending you their car – to help you on your quest to passing the driving test.

On the audio version of this book – which is essentially just me reading all this to you – the individual lessons run from just a few minutes up to about half-an-hour, with a total running time of about five hours. And, yeah, I know, that sounds like *ages* but, during a course of driving lessons, a professional instructor would spend just as much time working through these same lessons with you, but with the two of you often just parked at the side of the road.

Okay – fair enough – having covered a new lesson, a professional instructor would then help you to practise that lesson. But the *actual* lessons you're taken through are essentially universal. So, although every instructor likes to think of the way they teach as being unique, they all teach basically the same lessons.

They're the lessons in this book.

So, here we're going to cover the full syllabus, taught *systematically*, one thing at a time, building up your skills and knowledge in a structured way. Everything you need to know, all in simple everyday language – so nothing too technical…

Your clutch, for example, essentially works like a kitchen tap…

A tap controls the flow of water from the pipe to the sink – it can be dripping, or trickling, or gushing out – and your clutch controls the flow of **power** from the engine to the wheels in the same way as that tap controls the flow of water. So, explaining **clutch control** by saying it's you holding the clutch pedal nice-n-still just at the point where the power's **trickling** through to the wheels, will hopefully paint a picture you'll understand.

All the techniques and skills you must master, all the road and test knowledge you must know, it's all broken down into its component parts and laid out in the three sections of this book:

- **Section 1: Your car's controls and developing** *real* **control**
- **Section 2: Understanding the rules of the road and mastering traffic situations**
- **Section 3: What to expect from your Driving Examiner and what your Examiner will expect from you**

Everything you need.

It's all in this book.

So, if you're ready to go, let's get started, let's get into Lesson 1.

Enjoy.

MARK JOHNSTON

TOP GUN!

Lesson 1

Okay, so **Cockpit Drill**…sounds like you're heading off to flight school – a bit like *Top Gun* – to be a fighter pilot! But no, it's not quite as exciting as that – a car's cockpit drill is simply making sure that you're sitting nice and comfortably, and making sure the car's safe, before starting the engine.

So, first thing's first, check the doors are properly closed. Falling out of your car wouldn't be ideal on your driving test. Once that's done, organise your…

Seat Adjustment

You've usually got three adjustments you can make on a driver's seat. On some cars these will be controlled electronically, on others you'll have to physically move the seat about. Let's assume yours is just plain old manual, so no fancy electrics.

Start with the seat's height. It's obviously handy to be able to see through the windscreen, but hopefully without your head rubbing against the roof. To do this, you might find it's easier to get back out of the car, to take your weight off the seat, before adjusting it up. Manual adjusters work like a pump, so you literally pump the seat up. The handle to do this will usually be down between the base of your seat and the door. To set the seat height, unless you're really tall, start with the seat fully up, then, when you're back in the car, sitting comfortably, gently adjust the seat down, until it suits you.

Next, make sure you can reach the pedals comfortably. The lever to adjust the seat backwards and forwards is at the front of the seat, at the bottom near the floor, under one of your knees. Pull the lever to release the lock, then slide the seat forwards and backwards until you're able to press the clutch pedal – that's the one over to the left – all the way down, and to be able to hold it down comfortably, ideally with a slight bend at your knee. The lever is a simple locking mechanism, so it's usually best to take your foot off the clutch before you try to readjust the seat or else you might find yourself sliding backwards, and not able to reach the pedals at all. That's why it's not a good idea to attempt to adjust the seat whilst driving!

Then adjust the back of the seat for a comfortable reach to the steering wheel. There's usually a wheel or a lever down behind your hip that lets you move the back of the seat backwards and forwards. Then take hold of the steering wheel, imagining your hands to be at the ten-to-two position on a clock-face. Here you're looking for a slight bend at your elbows.

Finally, adjust the **head restraint**, commonly known as the **head rest**. The centre of the restraint should line up with your ears. There'll be a locking button, where the restraint meets the seat, that'll allow you to adjust it up and down.

The steering wheel may also have some potential adjustments. So if you're not comfortable holding the steering wheel where it is, you can often raise or lower it slightly, and it might also be possible to pull it back towards you. To do this, there's usually a handle down beneath the steering wheel that you simply pull out to release the clamp that holds it in position. You can then adjust it up or down, in or out, before pushing the locking handle back into place.

Okay, now let's set the...

Mirror Adjustment

Start by setting-up the *rear-view* mirror, that's the one in the centre of the windscreen. Firstly, notice that it has two fixed positions. If it's adjusted manually – again, some adjust electronically – then there's a lever behind the mirror that can be set to have the mirror pointing either up or down. You want it in the down position. This lever lets you flick your mirror glass up at night, if the car behind is dazzling you with its headlights. In this night-time *up* position you can still see following traffic, but without the glare.

Now, take hold of the outside of the mirror, its frame, not the glass – to keep your mucky fingerprints off – then move it around gently until you can see as much as possible through the back window. Start by lining up the bottom edge of the mirror with the bottom edge of the back window, with your hair or your seat's head restraint just visible in the right-hand side of the mirror. Then make any fine adjustments from there.

Then set the **door mirrors**. Again, they can be adjusted either manually or electronically, depending on your car. On the driver's side, set it so that you get the best possible view of the road, but with just a little bit of your own car in there too, just enough to give you some perspective between your car and any following traffic.

On the passenger side, do the same, except, when you've got it just right, tilt it down a fraction. You want it set so that you have a perfect view on that side of the car, but with just a hint of the kerb. It's really handy to have a slight view of the kerb – or the white line – when you're manoeuvring, parking in a bay, for example.

Now, with your door mirrors set, take a moment to find a reference point in each mirror, so that you can adjust your mirrors into exactly the same position again the next time you drive the car…

Now, what can you see?

Maybe the door handle is a couple of centimetres up from the bottom corner of the mirror, something like that, something you can remember and go back to. Anyway, having reference points will really help you, because by making sure you always have the mirrors set-up in the same way, you'll always have the same view of the kerb, or white line, to help you both manoeuvre accurately and also give you a consistent view of overtaking traffic.

Finally, you'll probably find that you'll want to readjust the mirrors occasionally during your first few drives, as you get comfortable with your new *personalised* driving position. But, like the seat, don't make those adjustments while you're actually driving. It's safer to stop the car first.

Okay, so your mirrors are set. But now, take just a quick peek over your right shoulder, then back to your door mirror, and try to work out what you **can't** see in the mirror. Then do the same with your left shoulder. The stuff that you can't see is in your **blind spots**. Maybe there's someone's driveway there or a parked car? Anyway, before moving away or changing lanes you'll need to glance – and it is just a quick glance – into one of those blind spots, just before you commit yourself to steering in that particular direction. It's really easy to lose sight of another vehicle in there, so your Driving Examiner will expect to see you making those checks on your driving test.

Now put your seatbelt on!

So, you now have your seat and mirrors adjusted, and your seatbelt on, so it's time to make sure the car's safe. This is called…

Securing The Car

And it simply means making sure the **handbrake's on and the gears are in neutral**.

Again, some car's have a fancy electronic handbrake, but assuming yours doesn't, to check the handbrake's on, gently pull up on the lever. If you hear a click-or-two then the handbrake wasn't fully on. But try not to heave up on the lever as though you're lifting a heavy suitcase, just a gentle pressure should do.

Then, to check the car's in its *neutral* gear position, take the gear lever and move it to either one side or the other – towards or away from you – then release it. The stick should spring back into the middle. That springy bit that you can feel is neutral. Like the handbrake, there's no need to wrench the gear-stick from side to side. Be gentle with it.

Now, I'll obviously be talking about the gears in detail in coming lessons, but for now, it's enough for you to know that neutral is like *zero* gear – so when your car's in neutral, even if the engine's running, it won't try to drive away.

And that's it. So, to sum up, the cockpit drill includes:

- Doors
- Seat
- Mirrors
- Seat belt
- Handbrake and Neutral checks

And that's you, settled into your car, ready to go.

MARK JOHNSTON

YOUR CAR'S CONTROLS & HOW TO USE THEM

In this lesson we'll introduce some of the characters in our car control story:

- Steering
- Handbrake
- Accelerator and Footbrake
- Clutch

The basic controls of a car haven't changed much in the past hundred years. But, of course, some car manufacturers haven't been able to leave the basics alone, so some cars might have a different type or position of handbrake, for example.

Anyway, the controls described in this lesson assume you're driving a *normal* car, one with an engine and a manual gearbox. Oh, and talking of gears, we'll not be getting into those just yet. We'll cover them in detail in Lesson 5, once we've got your car moving.

Okay, so let's get started. Let's talk about the…

Steering

Look at your steering-wheel. Place your hands on the wheel at ten-to-two, like the hands on a clock-face, same as you did when adjusting the seat. This is the way you're expected to hold it on your driving test, as it gives you maximum control of the steering. So, if a child ran out in front of you, and you needed to steer quickly, you'd pull the wheel down – giving you far more accurate control of the steering than if your hands were held low and you tried to push the wheel up.

Also, if you bumped into a pothole, those two strong hands of yours – balanced either side of the steering-wheel – would give you the best chance of keeping control. But, again, if your hands were low on the wheel, you could potentially have the steering-wheel ripped out of your hands. Not good.

Now, some drivers, when it comes to steering, just press one hand into the rim of the steering-wheel and spin it round, *palming* the wheel. While others, when, say, turning right, grip the wheel with their left hand then swing it over, past twelve o'clock to the three o'clock position, ***crossing their hands***.

Both of these techniques, while they can work just fine, involve that swing over the top of the wheel, where one or both hands pass over the twelve o'clock position. This is not the preferred style of steering on a driving test – although, nowadays, it won't actually be marked by an Examiner as a fault.

The ideal steering-technique for a driving test, so the one we'll be discussing, is known as ***feeding the wheel***.

Now, turning a steering-wheel in a stationary car, even one with powered steering, isn't good for it. It strains everything from the steering-wheel right down to the front tyres, and is called ***dry steering***. So when you're practising the movements of your hands around the wheel, don't actually turn the wheel unless the car's moving, just slide your hands around the outside of it. Or practise at home with a dinner plate. But an empty dinner plate, not the one with your dinner on it...

To get the feel of the way your hands should work as you steer, take hold of the wheel, hands at ten-to-two, and slide both hands up towards twelve o'clock. Then slide them both down towards six o'clock. And repeat. Try it for a moment. Slide both hands up to twelve, then both down to six. Twelve o'clock to six o'clock. Your hands always opposite one-another, one hand actually moving the wheel, the other simultaneously sliding round, following it – like a mirror image.

It takes practise. Most new drivers find this technique awkward at first. Stay with it. Keep practising. It might take a few goes, you may find that you'll need to do lots of laps of the car park, possibly even over several days, but you will get the hang of it.

Okay, so let's assume you've steered your car brilliantly around a corner, and now it's time to straighten it back up...

Some drivers simply loosen their grip on the steering wheel, allowing it to slide back through their hands. But on your driving test, your Examiner would like to see you use that same *feeding the wheel* method to take the steering back off again.

We'll discuss steering again in more detail, once we're ready to get the car moving, in Lesson 4, but now let's move onto the...

Handbrake

The handbrake's job is to hold the car still after you've stopped it with the footbrake. So the handbrake's not really designed to stop the car. However, having said that, if your footbrake ever failed – a scary thought – then pulling the handbrake on would stop you. But it wouldn't be a smooth stop. No, it'd be very abrupt, and it'd probably involve you skidding. But, in an emergency, it'd be better than nothing!

There are three reasons why your handbrake's not as good at stopping the car as the footbrake…

One: although your car has four brakes – one on each wheel – and your footbrake's connected to all four of them, your handbrake's only connected to the two at the back. So, trying to stop with the handbrake reduces your front brakes to useless spectators, leaving the rear brakes to do all the work.

Two: with your footbrake, you can have a little or a lot of stopping power, depending on how hard you press the brake pedal. But your handbrake doesn't have that level of control. It's just on or off. So when the handbrake's off your rear wheels are free to turn, but when it's on they're locked-up tight – which, if your car's moving, as we've already said, means you'll be skidding.

And three: the footbrake is connected to your car's ABS computer – the Anti-Lock Braking System – but your handbrake isn't. The ABS helps prevent you from skidding when you use the footbrake in an emergency or on a slippery road. The handbrake, though, as I said, isn't linked-up to the ABS, so if you pull it on while the car's moving, again, the back wheels will lock-up and the car will skid.

So, the footbrake's there to slow down and stop the car, and the handbrake's there to keep it still, like a ship's anchor.

By the way, when the handbrake's on, we say that it's *set*, and when it's off we say that it's been *released*.

The handbrake has three jobs. It's a…

- Parking brake
- Hill brake
- Safety brake

Let's add in some detail…

First, the handbrake's a *parking brake*. So, if you plan on exiting the car you'll need to set the handbrake first. If you forget, and you've parked on a hill…well, guess what'll happen.

Second, it's a *hill brake*. Say you've stopped at a red traffic light, facing uphill. You've got your footbrake on. Now, at last, a green light… So you need to get back on the accelerator to drive away again… Except, the moment you take your foot off the brake – if you haven't set the handbrake – you'll roll backwards, down the hill.

So, on a hill, stop with the footbrake, then set the handbrake to keep the car still. You can then move your foot from the brake to the accelerator, ready to go again, without having to worry about rolling back.

Finally, the handbrake's a *safety brake*. Maybe you're waiting to pull out of a petrol station, waiting for a bus to pass. Your feet are on the pedals, ready to go… But one of your feet slips and your car shoots forwards, completely out of control, right into the path of the bus. Nightmare…

But if the handbrake's on, and you slip off a pedal, your car won't move. The handbrake will hold you still and your engine will stall, it'll conk out.

So, to be on the safe side, if you're waiting for something – say, a bus to pass or a traffic light to change – then wait with the handbrake on. On test, having the handbrake on whenever you're stationary for any more than even a few seconds, will make your Examiner just that little bit more relaxed, and we all want a relaxed Examiner!

Now, if you look at a standard handbrake, you'll see that it has a button on top of the lever. That button connects to a catch, a lock, on the ratchet system that keeps the handbrake on. To release the brake, pull the lever up slightly – you'll see that the button pops in a few millimetres – then hold the button in while you lower the lever all the way down. Then release the button.

So, even though it only takes a second to release the handbrake, lots of new drivers try to rush it, letting go of the button before the lever's fully down. That means the brakes are still partially on. So, take your time, and make sure the lever's all the way down before letting go of the button.

Then, when you need to set the handbrake – again – use the button. Press it in, pull the lever up – and hold it up – until the button's released. A common mistake is to pull the lever up but to then release the pressure on the lever before releasing the button, allowing the lever to drop down slightly. So now the handbrake won't be fully on, so you could still potentially roll down that hill.

Another common mistake, when putting the handbrake on, is not using the button at all, giving you that annoying *clicking* sound. It's known as **ratcheting**. It doesn't really do any harm, but, yeah, it can be annoying. And, on test, try not to be annoying! Remember, we want your Examiner relaxed! So, hey, use the button!

Now, some cars have an electronic handbrake. It might take the form of a small lever. Flick the lever up and the handbrake's *set*. Easy. But releasing it could be a bit trickier because there will probably be two different ways of doing it.

The most common way is to simply ease the clutch up in readiness for moving away. Then, as the system *senses* you trying to move, it will automatically release the handbrake.

The other method, the one used less often, is to press the footbrake and flick the handbrake switch down. You'll be more likely to use this technique when moving away downhill.

Anyway, there are several different systems used by different car manufacturers, so take a moment to familiarise yourself with how yours works.

Okay, now let's move down to your foot controls, starting with your right foot, so that's the...

Accelerator And Footbrake

A manual car has three pedals, an automatic has just two. On a manual, the pedal over to the right is the accelerator, and the one in the middle is the brake. When you use these pedals, use them gently, with the ball of your foot, your heel on the floor.

Get used to the feel of the pedals with the engine switched off. Feel the way the accelerator moves easily all the way down, while the footbrake has a firmer feel. Practise moving your right foot across from one pedal to the other, without looking down.

Driving Instructors often call the accelerator the *gas* – I suppose mainly because we can say *gas* quicker than *accelerator*. But there's another reason. Calling it the accelerator might possibly make a new driver think it just makes the car go faster, to *accelerate*. But it's not. The gas works both ways...

So, yes, press it down and the car will accelerate, because you'll be pumping more fuel – gas – into the engine. But you also need to stay on the gas to keep your speed steady, adjusting your pressure on the pedal to deal with hills: more pressure as you climb up, less as you run down.

When you lift off the gas completely your car slows down, it *decelerates*. It's an effect known as *engine braking*. You're starving your engine of fuel, causing it to slow itself down. The use of engine braking is probably the best way to drive economically and smoothly. During engine braking, the system that pumps fuel into your engine closes down, so you're virtually driving for free.

Imagine you're approaching a roundabout. You can see a few cars in your lane, queuing up. You're still a fair bit away from the roundabout, but at this point, you lift off the gas pedal – even though you're not going to brake just yet – to begin using engine braking. Immediately, you'll feel your car settle, gently slowing itself down, giving the cars ahead of you more time to get moving, giving you more time to plan your approach to the roundabout. Then, after maybe five or ten seconds of this nice, smooth engine-braking, you can use your footbrake – if necessary – for the final approach to the roundabout.

Looking ahead like this, easing off the gas when you can see that you're going to have to slow down for something, is known in driving books as **accelerator sense**. Though a better name for it is probably just **common sense**! The idea is that when you see a problem up ahead, ideally you should ease up off the accelerator, to begin gently slowing down, before using the footbrake...

Which is the middle pedal...

Remember, the footbrake connects to all four brakes, one on each wheel. The technique to use the footbrake smoothly is known as **progressive braking**...

Think of applying the footbrake over a scale of one to five – *one* being a gentle squeeze, *five* pressing the brake down hard. Braking progressively is applying the brakes to a count of one... two...three. Then, just before you stop, ease progressively back up off the brake: three...two... so that as you finally stop, the pressure on the footbrake's back at number one, barely touching the pedal at all.

Braking progressively means you'll stop nice-n-smoothly. But if you come to a stop with the footbrake still down at, say, number three, then you'll stop abruptly, and everything on the back seat – possibly including your passengers – will fall on the floor!

Okay, so that's the gas and the footbrake. They're pretty

straightforward, so it's easy to get your head round what they both do, but in a car with a manual gearbox, the...

Clutch

...is trickier, because sometimes when you press the clutch pedal down the car slows down, but other times it speeds up. *Oh dear...*

So let's try to clear this contradiction up. And, to do that, let's start by picturing a bicycle...

A bicycle works by the rider turning the pedals which turns the chain which turns the gears which, finally, turns the wheel. Then off goes our cyclist, merrily down the road. So the power from the bicycle's pedals is linked to the gears – then onto the back wheel – by the chain.

So a bicycle works by...

- Pedals
- Chain
- Gear
- Wheel

Now picture the workings of a car. There's an engine, which turns the clutch, which turns the gears, which turns the wheels.

So a car works by...

- Engine
- Clutch
- Gears
- Wheels

A car's clutch, then, does a similar job as a bicycle's chain. It connects the power to the wheels, via the gears. But the big difference between the two is that the clutch can be controlled: pressing the clutch pedal down **breaks the chain**, it prevents the engine's power from getting to the wheels.

You see, when a cyclist wants to stop the flow of power to the back wheel of their bike they simply stop pedalling. But a driver can't do that – their engine keeps *pedalling*, keeps producing power. In fact, the only way to stop it producing power is to switch it off, which, particularly if you're only stopping briefly, wouldn't be particularly convenient!

So a car driver needs a way of preventing the power their engine's continually producing from getting to the wheels. They need to be able to break the chain – to break the connection – between the engine and the wheels. And that's exactly what happens when the clutch pedal is pressed down.

Okay, so let's go back to the bicycle, the rider happily pedalling along on a nice level country lane. Now, what happens when they stop pedalling? Does the bike stop dead in its tracks, throwing them over the handlebars?

Well, no, it doesn't stop, not immediately anyway. Instead it just kind of rolls along for a while, carried by momentum. It's called *freewheeling*...

And what happens when our freewheeling cyclist meets a hill?

Well, uphill their bike will stop much sooner than on a level road. But downhill, especially if it's steep, their bike will speed up as it rolls all the way down to the bottom of the hill.

A freewheeling bicycle, then, is controlled by the gradient: uphill it stops, downhill it speeds up.

So how does this relate to your car?

Well, remember, at the start of this section we said that sometimes when you press the clutch pedal down your car stops but at other times it speeds up?

Well, that's because when you're driving along and you press the clutch down, just like that bicycle, your car's now freewheeling. And also, just like the bicycle, when your car's freewheeling it goes with the gradient: uphill it'll stop but downhill it'll speed up. So your car's simply rolling along – freewheeling – like a rollercoaster ride!

Oh, and another thing, when a car's freewheeling – just to confuse things – it's not called freewheeling. Oh no, that'd be far too easy! In a car it's called *coasting*.

So, when a car's coasting, it's simply rolling, so...

- **Uphill it slows down**
- **Downhill it speeds up**

Now, there are just three occasions when you need to press the clutch down. They are to...

- Coast
- Stop
- Change gear

Let's look at them in detail...

Number one, then, is to coast. This is done at very low speed, usually only in 1st or 2nd gear.

Let's say you just want your car to gently ease along those last few metres up to a T-junction at the end of a road. Now, on a bicycle, in that situation, you'd simply stop pedalling, use the brakes as necessary, and let the bike freewheel up to the junction.

Well, it's the same idea in your car. So – rather than having the engine drive you right up to the junction – for those last couple of car lengths, use the brake and simply press the clutch down to coast up.

Number two is to stop. Generally, to stop a car, you use the footbrake to slow down, then, just before actually stopping, you'd press the clutch down as well. So, to stop a car, you need two feet: one on the brake, one on the clutch.

But that doesn't mean the clutch is a *kind of* brake. Remember, downhill the car will speed up when the clutch goes down. So the idea is to make sure you have the car under control with the brake **before** the clutch goes down.

Finally, number three, is to press the clutch down to change gear. Er…self-explanatory, this one, I think.

Mistakes? Well, the main one is, always pressing the clutch down while braking. Braking, you'll remember, isn't on our list of the three occasions when you need the clutch.

Stopping, though, is. And that's where the confusion lies. So, if you're braking – just slowing down a bit – you don't need the clutch. But if you brake right down to the point where you're about to stop, it's then that you press the clutch down.

Oh, and when you do press that clutch pedal down, give it a good quick push, nice-n-positive. That way you'll get a clean break between the engine and the gears. There's no need to press the clutch down slowly.

So, we've discussed what happens when you press the clutch pedal down, and we've discussed the three occasions when you'll need to do it. But what about lifting the clutch pedal up, what happens then?

Well, when you lift the clutch pedal, you re-connect the engine to the wheels.

When lifting the clutch, if possible, try to keep your heel on the floor. If you keep your heel grounded you're lifting the clutch by flexing your ankle and lifting your toes, allowing you the subtle movements needed for clutch control. But if you allow your heel to rise up, then you're trying to control the clutch by flexing your hip, which is a whole lot trickier!

However, note that keeping your heel down is much easier if your shoe size is closer to a ten than a five!

Okay, so lifting the clutch pedal up... If your car's moving, and you've had the clutch down, say, for a gear change, then lift it back up over a count of three: one...two...three.

Lifting the clutch gently in this way gives you a nice smooth transition from the clutch being down and the car **coasting**, to the clutch being back up and it being *driven* by the engine again. If you ease the clutch pedal back up, over that count of three, after a gear change, all you'll be aware of is a slight change in the sound of the engine, you won't actually *feel* anything. But if you lift the clutch abruptly then the car will shudder and lurch.

And what about using the clutch to get a stationary car moving?

Two things....

- Your clutch is essentially a tap
- And it comes up in two stages, with a pause in between

Hang on! A clutch is a tap?

Okay, so picture a water tap. Say, a bathroom tap. It allows you to control the flow of water from the pipe into the sink. Turn the tap just one turn, nothing happens. But turn it a little more and you get a drip. A little more still, and you get a trickle. Until, finally, the tap's fully open and the water's gushing out.

Well, your clutch is also a tap, except this one controls the flow of power from your engine to your gears – then onto the wheels – but it does it in the same way as the one in your bathroom controls the flow of water.

When the clutch pedal is held down, the tap is turned off, so no power flows. But then, as you lift the clutch pedal – like opening a tap – eventually you'll get a drip – **a drip of power** – making its way through to the wheels. Then, as you lift the clutch higher, that drip becomes a trickle until, when the pedal's all the way up, the power's pouring through, driving you along.

Your bathroom tap gives you complete control over the flow of water. Your clutch gives you complete control over the flow of power.

When you're moving, say, out of a parking space, to keep things under control, hold the clutch pedal still at the point where the power's *trickling* through to the wheels, with your car barely moving. You have control over the flow of power. You have *clutch control*.

You see, your engine's a big bully – it wants to shove you around – but your clutch keeps the bully in check, taming it…

The engine *produces* the power but the clutch *controls* the power.

And number two – so the second thing to think about in relation to using the clutch to get your car moving – is that a clutch comes up in two stages, with a very definite pause of a couple of seconds in between those stages.

And we'll be discussing both of those aspects to using the clutch in the next lesson.

I think that's almost a *cliffhanger*…

MOVING AWAY
AND STOPPING

Lesson 3

This lesson refers to moving away in a car with a manual gearbox, and includes a few sequences that you'll be using when actually driving, as well as some practical exercises. If you plan on practising them, please make sure you do so legally and safely.

Let's start by talking a bit more about the gas and the clutch, and about the all-important **biting point**. Then we'll move on to discussing:

- The simple secret to avoid ever stalling your engine
- Moving away on a level road
- Stalling
- Braking and stopping from higher speeds
- Moving away safely

But first, some revision…

In Lesson 1, when discussing *cockpit drill*, and ensuring the car's *secure*, we mentioned that neutral is *zero* gear. If the car's in neutral – even if the engine's running – it won't drive off.

Also, remember that to check your car's in neutral, move the gear-stick sideways – towards or away from you – then just let it spring back to its central, neutral, position. The way that spring pulls the gear-stick into the centre is known as the gearbox **bias**.

The bias in most modern gearboxes has the gear-stick sitting directly between third and fourth gears. So from neutral, if you were to simply push the gear-stick forward, you'd shift into third.

Before starting your engine, always check the gear-stick – and that spring – to make sure you're in neutral, and also check that the handbrake's on.

Okay, revision class over, let's move on, and talk in a little more detail about using the accelerator – the gas – when moving away…

Does your car have a *rev-counter*?

The rev-counter's job is to let you know how fast the internals of your engine are spinning – how many revolutions of the moving parts there are in any given minute – known as *Revs per Minute*, or **RPM**. And your engine spins really fast. Those single-digit numbers on the rev-counter have to be multiplied by a thousand. So when it shows '3' on the dial, your engine's spinning at three thousand times a minute – that's fifty times a second!

Imagine you started your engine and let it run at *tick-over*, or *idle*. Let's say it idles at 800RPM. Now, to produce enough power to actually move your car, you're going to have to *set the gas*. That involves bringing the RPM up to, say, 1500 by very gently pressing the accelerator – the gas pedal – while keeping an eye on the rev-counter, then keeping the gas pedal nice-n-still.

At this point, at 1500RPM, you'll hear the engine making a lively, *humming* sound. Your engine's now producing enough power to easily move the weight of your car – even if you're facing uphill with members of your local rugby club onboard!

Remember, though, that although the gas **produces** the power, it's the clutch that **controls** the flow of that power – like a tap – to the wheels. So let's delve a little deeper into understanding the workings of the clutch…

Your left foot operates the clutch pedal. At the other end of the clutch mechanism from the clutch pedal is a *friction plate* which, strangely enough, is known as a *clutch plate*. Its job is to grip – to *clutch* – onto the *flywheel*.

The flywheel is a steel disc the size of a dinner plate that is spun around by the engine: the faster the flywheel spins, the higher the RPM, the more power the engine produces,

Imagine you're in your car, engine running, in gear, and you're holding the clutch pedal down. When the clutch is down, essentially what's happening is that you're holding the clutch plate away from the spinning flywheel…

But then, as you lift the clutch pedal, strong springs push the friction plate towards the flywheel, closing the gap between them, until eventually – *contact* – the friction plate and the flywheel meet. This contact is called the *biting point*, also known as *the bite*. It's the point where the *tap* has been opened enough to allow a gentle drip of power to make its way through to the wheels.

At the bite, the sound of your engine changes, like a weightlifter sucking in air preparing for a heavy lift. Deep down in the engine, the friction plate has started to clutch onto the flywheel. But it hasn't fully gripped it yet, the bite is only the initial contact. So the bite is *not* the point where the bonnet lifts or the back squats. If your car does react like that, if it feels like it's desperately trying to move, then the clutch pedal is up too high – above the bite – so squeeze it back down a touch.

To find the bite, you must feel how your car's reacting and also listen to the sound of the engine.

However, the change in the sound of your engine depends on the electrical system employed in your car. In older cars, as you come to the bite, the engine note **drops**, because you're asking the engine to start doing some actual work. But, on modern cars, the engine note **rises** as some electrical wizardry in the engine works-out what you're about to do so feeds a little more fuel to the engine in readiness for moving away.

Nothing's ever straightforward, is it?

Anyway, this all sounds pretty simple: listen to the sound of your engine then keep your clutch foot still. But keeping your clutch pedal nice-n-still when you're in a tight spot – keeping it just at that point where the car's moving under control – is the essence of low-speed car control.

This, then, is the breakdown for initially finding your clutch's biting point:

- Clutch in
- 1st gear
- Lift the clutch gently and slowly
- **Listen and feel for** *the bite*
- Keep both feet still for five seconds…
- Then, clutch back down to the floor
- Keep your feet still
- Secure the car by moving the gear-stick back into neutral and making sure the handbrake's still on
- Relax your feet

Now try that again but with power, so with *setting the gas*:

- Clutch in
- 1st gear
- *Set the Gas*
- Lift the clutch gently and slowly
- **Listen and feel for** *the bite*
- Keep both feet still for five seconds…
- **Come off the gas**
- Clutch back down to the floor
- Keep your feet still
- Secure the car by moving the gear-stick back into

neutral and making sure the handbrake's still on
• Relax your feet

So, preparing to move away by finding the bite, goes:

• Clutch down
• 1st gear
• Set the gas
• Find the bite

If you get chance to practise this, get your Supervisor to park on a level area of a car park and try the following exercise...

Now, it's REALLY important to lift the clutch pedal slowly, then to keep it still again the moment you feel movement.

So:

• Clutch down
• 1st gear
• Keep the clutch down
• Handbrake off
• Keep the clutch down
• **Now, very slowly, ease the clutch up...**
• Try to listen and feel for the bite
• **Clutch up a little further until you feel movement...**
• **KEEP THE CLUTCH STILL**
• Creep forward for a couple of seconds
• Then clutch down
• Touch footbrake and stop
• Keep both feet still
• Secure the car
• Relax your feet

Now let's move onto talking about what happens as you lift the clutch pedal up beyond the bite, and let's discuss a favourite lesson of mine...

The Simple Secret To Avoid Ever Stalling Your Engine

So, the secret to avoid stalling the engine, and also to moving away smoothly and under control, is to move away by firstly lifting the clutch up to the biting point, but then to bring it up fully in two further stages, with a definite pause of a couple of seconds between those two final stages.

So the idea is to bring the clutch up gently to the bite. Then, when you're ready to drive away, to ease the clutch up a wee bit further until you feel the car moving, **then to keep the clutch still for a couple of seconds**, before easing it up again fully for the final stage.

The idea is to bring the clutch up slowly – to control it – right up to the point where the clutch pedal stops and you simply lift your foot away from it. **At no point do you lift the clutch abruptly.**

Those crucial couple of seconds between these final two stages give your engine chance to get the weight of the car moving...

Imagine a friend's car has broken down and they've asked you for a push. Would you run headlong at their car like an angry rhino, charging into it, trying to move it in one mad rush? Or would you get your body behind it, to gently move it – starting slowly – easing it forward?

Well your engine feels the same way. It wants to be given time to get the car's weight moving.

So, to move away smoothly on a level road – release the handbrake – then:

- Ease the clutch up to the bite
- Then up a little higher, until the car starts to move

- Then keep the clutch still for a couple of seconds
- Finally, ease it all the way up

We've already talked about thinking of the clutch as a tap. And I'm going to push the analogy even further now by using it to help describe the three stages over which you lift up the clutch pedal, the three stages that see the power flowing from the engine to the wheels:

- Stage 1: the bite – is a *drip* of power
- Stage 2: the car begins to move – is a *steady trickle* of power
- Then keep the clutch still for those couple of seconds...
- Stage 3: the clutch comes all the way up – the power is *gushing* through

This next sequence is moving away and stopping using those three clutch stages:

- Clutch down
- First gear
- Set the gas
- Clutch Stage 1: find the bite
- Now, release the handbrake...
- Clutch Stage 2: ease it up until the car moves
- Keep both feet still for a couple of seconds
- Clutch Stage 3: ease it up fully
- Let the car drive for a couple of car lengths...
- Then, clutch all the way down to begin coasting
- Gently use the footbrake to stop
- Keep both feet still
- Secure the car – that's handbrake and neutral
- Relax your feet

Let's tighten that sequence up a little:

- Clutch in
- First gear

- Set the gas
- Clutch 1: the bite
- Feet still
- Handbrake off
- Clutch 2: ease it up until you're moving
- Keep both feet still for a couple of seconds
- Clutch 3: ease it all the way up
- Drive for a bit…
- Then, clutch down
- Footbrake and stop
- Secure the car
- Relax

In these early stages you're trying to achieve four things:

- You're coordinating your feet to balance the gas and the bite
- You're feeling the way the clutch makes the car move as you ease it up over the three stages
- You're practising keeping your feet still for those crucial couple of seconds between each of the three stages
- You're getting used to coasting

Any problems?

- If you're *stalling* the engine (see below) then you're bringing the clutch up either too far or too fast
- If you're jumping forward then you're possibly lifting off the final part of the clutch pedal's movement too abruptly. Remember, keep the pedal under control until *it* stops, then lift your foot away from the pedal
- If you stall as you're braking then you're braking before getting the clutch down
- If you stop abruptly, you're braking too heavily. Gently does it

Now, if you're able to practise the above exercise, that's great.

Hopefully you'll get the hang of it within a couple of goes. So... job done? No, definitely not! Once it feels like you've got the hang of it, do it another hundred times! This skill must be virtually second nature before you venture out on the road, especially if you're going to be driving your own car, or any other car that doesn't have dual controls.

Okay, those are the four things you're working on, but sometimes things don't go according to plan, and one of those occasions is...

Stalling

Stalling is when your engine cuts out accidentally. When you stall, the engine will fall silent, the rev-counter will drop to zero, and various warning lights on your dashboard will light up. *Houston, we have a problem...*

And that problem is most likely to happen when you're moving away, because, as you now know, moving away requires you to coordinate the gas, the clutch and the handbrake, so it takes a lot of practise.

But if you do stall, don't panic! Even the best of us stall occasionally. The most important thing is to make sure you keep your car under control, **that you keep it still**, and that it doesn't start rolling away from you.

So, you need a brake, preferably the handbrake. Then, either with the clutch pedal held down or with the gear-stick in neutral, re-start the engine.

If your car has *Stop / Start* then make sure you have a brake on before pressing the clutch back down to re-start the engine. If you don't, when the clutch goes down, you will start to roll.

Remember, you will also stall if you don't press the clutch down just before stopping.

To stop in first gear, as discussed in the above sequences, **press the clutch down first**, then lift off the gas and get your right foot over to the brake. That way you'll slow down and stop nice-n-smoothly.

But when you're...

Braking And Stopping From Higher Speeds

...the idea is to **come off the gas first**, to begin *engine braking*, then use the footbrake *progressively*, and then – when the car's slowing right down and you've got it nicely under control – to press the clutch down.

So:

- In first gear: press the clutch down, then come off the gas, then brake
- But in the higher gears: come off the gas, then brake, then press the clutch down, as you prepare to stop

Okay, so far we've dealt with the physical act of controlling the car when moving away, but that's only half the story – the second part involves...

Moving Away Safely

To begin the next part of the moving away sequence, let's first think about looking in the rear-view mirror for any approaching traffic. The idea is to *give-way* to that traffic coming up behind you, to give them *priority*.

To give-way means to not inconvenience other drivers, so not forcing them to either slow down for you or to have to steer around you.

When it's clear in the rear-view mirror, indicate. The indicator is to warn people in front of you that you're about to start driving towards them.

Then glance to your blind-spot – that area alongside the car that the mirrors don't cover. If you're moving away from the left-hand kerb, check your right-hand blind-spot. If you're leaving the right-hand kerb, check your left-hand blind-spot.

Finally, watch for any approaching traffic in your door mirror. The situation can change quickly, so you need to keep one eye in the mirror as you prepare to move away. Then, once you've run through the safety procedure, it's time to release the handbrake, ease the clutch up over its second two stages, and drive away.

So the full moving away procedure has **ten**, yes, **TEN** parts! And it goes like this:

- Clutch in
- 1st gear
- Set the gas
- Find the bite
- Mirror
- Signal
- (grab hold of the handbrake)
- Blind-spot check
- Door mirror
- Release the handbrake
- Clutch stages 2 and 3

So the full procedure for moving away and then stopping again, on a level road, goes like this:

- Clutch in
- 1st gear
- Set the gas
- Clutch 1: find the bite
- Mirror
- Signal

- (grab the handbrake)
- Blind-spot
- Door mirror
- Clutch 2: up until you feel movement
- Keep your clutch still for a couple of seconds
- Clutch 3: all the way up
- Drive with the gas pedal for a couple of car lengths…
- Then, clutch down
- Footbrake and stop
- Secure the car
- Relax

It's two feet to move the car and two feet to stop it again. Simply taking your foot off the gas doesn't stop you. It slows you down, yes, but to stop the car you need to press the clutch down and brake, otherwise you'll just keep on going!

Practise, practise, practise. This stuff is the foundation for everything you'll ever do in the car.

Don't rush onto the next lesson until you've got this one *down*. Moving away and stopping is such an important part of driving and your driving test. Your Examiner will get you to pull over and move away again several times. So come back here, and revise this lesson, the night before your test!

Now, remember, there's no rush, but when you're ready, I'll see you in Lesson 4 for some steering practise…

STEERING

Lesson 4

Now that you can start and stop the car, it's time to find yourself a huge empty space to try your hand – well, both hands, hopefully – at steering. An airport runway would be nice, but you're probably going to have to make do with a quiet, early-morning car park.

Steering takes priority over the other hand controls. The last thing you want, halfway round a corner, is to take your focus off the steering and move your concentration on to, say, the gears or the indicators. Do the steering first.

As discussed in previous lessons, have your hands on the wheel at roughly a ten-to-two position, to give you quick accurate steering and a good firm grip on the wheel. Also, remember that the steering technique you'll be using as you build towards your driving test is called *feeding the wheel*. This is where you keep both hands on their own side of the wheel, your hands opposite one-another, working between the top of the wheel – twelve o'clock – and the bottom of the wheel – six o'clock. Then, once you've finished the turn, use that same technique to straighten up again.

So, steering to the right, move your right hand up towards the twelve o'clock position, grip the wheel and pull it down. At the same time, slide your left hand down the other side of the wheel, so that both hands meet at six o'clock. Then, from there, grip the wheel with your left hand and push the wheel up, this time with your right hand sliding up the wheel, until both hands meet again at twelve.

Phew!

To turn left it's the opposite. Start by reaching up slightly with your left hand, then grip the wheel and pull it down, while at the same time sliding your right hand down, until they meet at six.

It's normal to find this technique tricky to get the hang of, but try to keep at it. However, having said that, although this is the preferred steering technique for a driving test, nowadays your Examiner won't be too concerned if you stray from it and, say, allow your hands to *cross.* Essentially, provided you're steering safely and accurately – using both hands – your Examiner won't mark you down on a test, whichever technique you use.

Before practising, get your Supervisor to demonstrate a couple of things for you. Well three things, actually…

First, that the area you have to work in is big enough. From your starting position, you want to be able to drive around in a big oval shape, to be able to steer to ***full lock*** – that's the point where the steering wheel won't turn any further, which on most cars is about one-and-a-half full turns of the wheel – and have enough room for the car to be able to turn all the way back on itself, so that you're facing back in the opposite direction.

The trick is to get the steering on nice-n-quickly, but then to be a bit more relaxed as you take the steering off again.

The second thing you want your Supervisor to demonstrate – ideally – is the *feeding the wheel* steering technique that you'll hopefully be using. Now, this might be easier said than done, it might be that your Supervisor hasn't used this technique in years, in which case you can sit back and enjoy watching them tying themselves in knots! But do watch – carefully – because as you watch them coming to terms with the technique it'll help you pick it up, too.

The third thing is that, once it's moving – provided you're on a level *road* – with the clutch pedal up, even if you don't touch the gas, the car will just keep on going. This means that once the car's moving you'll be able to focus on your steering technique without having to control the gas pedal.

Remember, though, that you need two feet to stop again!

Okay, so the demonstration we'd like to see from your Supervisor is: moving away then settling into the speed that it'll do on tick-over, just pulling itself slowly along without using the gas pedal. Then you want to see that you have plenty of room for the steering practise, room to drive around the car park in a big oval shape.

Notice that, especially in a straight line, you don't really steer the car with your hands, you steer it with your eyes – **the car goes where you look**. After all, you don't look at the handlebars when you're riding your bike, do you? No, you look where you're going. It's the same here.

Also note that the faster you go the more responsive your steering becomes. At 1st gear speeds you'll need to turn the wheel a lot to get the car to turn, but when you go faster the car steers with just the slightest movement of the wheel.

So, on the open road, at higher speeds, look well ahead, and look where you want to go. Try not to look down at the road right in front of you. That'd be like walking along the High Street staring down at your feet.

In Lesson 2, we discussed dry steering – turning the wheel while stationary – and said that it can lead to excessive wear-n-tear on your car's steering. But there's another reason to avoid dry-steering. If you turn the wheel while stationary at, say, a junction, then you'll lose track of where you'll end up going when you do finally drive off...

So, turning left, leaving a side road, for example, if you turn the wheel while you're waiting for a gap in traffic, when you do finally get chance to move you're likely to bump straight into the kerb, because you'll have steered in too much.

And finally, note that when you steer sharply at low speed, the back of your car **doesn't** exactly follow the front. No, your back wheels take a short cut. Have you ever noticed the way a lorry driver swings his truck around a corner? When turning left at, say, traffic lights, the front of the truck seems to go miles forward before the driver turns, yet the truck's back wheels barely miss the kerb.

Well, your car does the same thing, though not quite as dramatically as that huge truck. So, when you're coming forwards out of a space in a busy car park, you need to get at least half of your car out of the space before turning the wheel, otherwise the back of your car will scrape the car alongside you. **As a rough guide, remember to get your shoulders out of the parking space before steering sharply.**

And, if you're turning into a side road where there's a really sharp turn, same thing: get your shoulders up to the start of the turn then steer in quickly. This technique will keep you on your own side of the road – provided you're driving slowly – but without your back wheel bumping up the kerb.

Anyway, now it's time for you to swap places with your Supervisor and try your hands at some steering practise. The plan is to use the moving away technique from the previous lesson to get yourself moving slowly in a straight line, then...

- Off the gas, and let the car move on tick-over
- Now, steer round to the right (or left) until you turn all the way around and face back up the car park
- Remember, try to put the steering on quickly, then take it off again slowly

- Straighten up
- Drive along with the gas for a bit
- Then off the gas again and let the engine settle back down to tick-over
- Steer fully back round to the right (or left) again
- Straighten up
- Drive back to the start position
- Clutch down
- Footbrake
- Stop
- Secure the car – handbrake and neutral

And again, lots of practise. It's absolutely crucial that you're able to comfortably move away, steer and stop before heading out onto the road.

Well, that's it from Lesson 4. In Lesson 5, we'll shift up and ROCK!

MARK JOHNSTON

GEARS ARE TO CARS WHAT GUITARS ARE TO ROCK 'N' ROLL

Lesson 5

(Apologies to our *automatic* readers for the lesson title!)

This is the best bit: shifting gear. If you're able to practise this lesson, start by heading back to your favourite car park. You're going to need a straight run, at least the length of a football pitch, to give you room to practise a gear change or two.

Now, we're going to be talking about:

- Finding your way
- What each gear does and when to change
- How to change gear
- Using the gears on hills
- Changing down to go faster
- The mistakes people make

Let's begin with the position of each gear, and a section we'll call...

Finding Your Way

In previous lessons, we've met **neutral** – that we think of as **zero** *gear* – and 1st gear, the one we use for moving away and for low-speed manoeuvring.

Now, from the driver's seat, with the engine off and the clutch pedal held down, take hold of the gear-stick. Remember that to check the car's in neutral, you either pull the stick gently towards you or push it away. Either way, in neutral, it'll spring back into that central position.

Take a look at the stick. Most have a diagram on the **gear-knob** (I know, I know! Get over it). It's a map of where each gear's situated, known as the **gate.** Feel beneath the gear-knob to the metal bar connecting it to the car itself. It's often buried beneath a cover of a soft, plastic fabric that's pretending to be leather, and it's usually the length and thickness of a pencil.

Now, look back down at the gate, at the map of the gears. Imagine you're in 4th gear and you want to change into 2nd. To get from 4th, you must move the stick up, into neutral, then follow the line across to the left, then down into 2nd. There are no short cuts. There are no diagonals.

Try it. Be gentle. Move the stick around between the gears. Feel the spring. Feel the way you follow the gate to find each gear. And find reverse...

Different cars have different ways of **protecting** reverse – after all, we don't want you accidentally driving backwards! Some have it all the way over to the right, away from 1st gear. Some have it next to 1st with, perhaps, a lever beneath the gear-knob that you pull up to find reverse.

Feel how 1st and 2nd gears are over to the left, and 5th over to the right. But also feel how you can't find the middle of the gate, how you have to let the spring settle the gear-stick into its neutral position, for both 3rd and 4th.

So, 3rd is *over to the right* of 2nd, but it's not *completely* over to the right – you don't have to pull it across - it's in the middle of

the gate.

So, when you take the gear-stick out of 2nd to change into 3rd, simply relax your grip, and let the stick settle into its neutral position – then gently push it forward into 3rd.

From 1st gear into 2nd you must hold the stick over to the left. With the stick in 1st, try rolling your hand around the gear-knob so that your palm is facing away from you, towards your Supervisor, then scoop the stick back into 2nd, as if you were scooping nice warm bathwater around yourself on a winter's night. But notice that, if you don't use the scoop technique, how easy it is for the stick to accidentally spring across and fall into 4th gear.

Now, remaining stationary, change up through the gears, 1st to 5th. Then try it without looking down. Picture the position of each gear, picture the map. Remember there are no shortcuts or diagonals – it's all side to side, forward and back. Feel the movement of the stick. Work *against* the spring for 1st and 2nd, keeping the stick over to the left. But, then, for 3rd and 4th, work *with* the spring, letting it settle into its neutral position. Gentle movements. Don't force the stick or move it abruptly. Relax with it.

Then go down through the gears. Firstly in sequence: 5th, 4th, 3rd, 2nd then back into 1st. But, then out of sequence, so from 4th, say, back to 2nd.

Okay, so now you've got the feel of the position of each gear, let's talk a little bit about…

What Each Gear Does And When To Change

1st gear you've already met. It's there for moving away and for low speed control. So leaving a parking space or a driveway is done in 1st. Then, as the car speeds up, you change up through the gears in sequence, deciding when to change up based on the **sound** of the engine. We all know *that* engine noise kids make, playing with cars… *Brrrmmm!*

So, as you speed up, you change up, generally in sequence, based on the sound of the engine.

Around town, in thirty limits, in most cars you really only need 1st, 2nd and 3rd, as 3rd gear and 30mph usually suit each other perfectly. If you want to use 4th around town, be careful, because in 4th many cars will *want* to go faster than thirty, and on your driving test your Examiner will be far more concerned about the speed you're doing than the gear you're using.

Also, many folk talk about *getting up into fourth as soon as possible*, to save fuel. But the most economical gear for any given situation is the one that gives you the most control. It's all about control. If you're driving well, you're driving economically.

Also, remember that although many people might say they use 4th in thirty limits, they might not actually be driving at thirty! They might be driving at 20% over the speed limit, and that won't be acceptable on your test.

Anyway, cars differ. For all I know you might be learning to drive in an Aston Martin. So, when you start driving on the road, discuss it with your Supervisor and see which gear feels most comfortable to use when you're at thirty.

Now, changing down. Two things…

First, although we generally change up in sequence, **changing down is done** *selectively*.

Selective gear changing means, rather than simply changing down in sequence, instead, change down directly into the gear you're actually planning on using next.

In other words, changing down, leave gears out.

Now, changing up selectively *is* okay, say, 2nd up into 4th – perhaps when you're going down a steep hill or if you've accelerated **briskly** in 2nd – it won't do your car any harm, but it's done far less frequently than when changing down, to the point where most drivers never do it at all.

But changing down, it's normal to be shifting from, say, 4th gear into 2nd, or from 3rd into 1st. In fact, if the situation calls for it, you might even find yourself changing down directly from *top gear* into 1st.

Second thing: although we change **up** based on the sound of the engine, **changing down is based on miles-per-hour, so based on the speed that you're actually doing.**

As a rough guide, round up your speed in miles-per-hour then take away the zero. So, as we've already said, in most cars 30mph suits 3rd gear.

Forty suits 4th. Twenty suits 2nd…

But each gear then has a **range** of speeds that it works over. So 3rd gear doesn't only work at thirty. No, its range is from about 15mph *below* thirty all the way up to 15mph *above* thirty. So, 3rd gear works from 15mph all the way up to forty-five, with thirty being the middle of its range.

Using this system, 2nd gear's range is from just above walking pace, up through twenty, all the way up to 35mph.

4th works from twenty-five up to fifty-five.

So, at 30mph, your car would be happy in any of three gears – 2nd, 3rd or 4th – but it would be happiest in 3rd.

Again, this is only a guide, so discuss it with your Supervisor and then, when you're out on the road, see how your car feels…

Try cruising along in 2nd at 20mph… Then come off the gas and let the speed fade away to as slow as feels comfortable for the engine… Then accelerate, up past twenty, to as fast as feels comfortable. That's your car's range in 2nd.

Okay, so now we know the theory of which gear to choose, let's talk about…

How To Change Gear

But just before we do, bear in mind three things…

First: the most important thing to remember during a gear change is to keep looking where you're going…

Don't look down!

Remember, you steer with your eyes, not with your hands. So if, during a gear change, you start looking down at the gear-stick, trying to figure-out what to do next, you will likely end up in somebody's hedge!

Second thing: if you were to time a gear change as if it were an Olympic sport then the stopwatch would start when you press the clutch pedal down, **not** when you take hold of the gear-stick. Taking hold of the gear-stick is simply preparation for the gear change to come…

So, when changing gear, say to yourself: *hand down, clutch down…*

- **Hand down to the gear-stick in preparation**
- **Clutch down to begin the actual gear change**

Finally, third thing: when the clutch is down for the gear change, make sure your foot is off the gas. Generally, if you're changing down this won't be a problem because you'll already be off the gas, slowing the car down…

But, changing up, the sequence now becomes:

- **Hand down**

- **Clutch down**
- **Off the gas**

If you don't lift off the gas at this point your engine will get really noisy. It won't do it any harm, but it will scream its head off at you in complaint, and quite possibly, so will your Supervisor!

Anyway, let's work through changing up from 1st gear into 2nd. Oh, and take your time. Focus on the sequence. Don't try to rush things. Your gear changes will soon quicken up, but for now, focus on the sequence. So:

- In a straight line, accelerate gently in 1st gear
- Listen to the sound of the engine
- Reach down (but don't look down!) to find the gear-stick
- Remember, cup your hand around the gear-knob, ready to hold the stick over to the left
- Clutch down
- Lift off the gas
- Scoop the stick back, holding it to the left, to change gear
- Clutch up gently, over a count of 1...2...3...
- Back on the gas

At the end of the gear change, if you want the car to slow down, leave the gas pedal alone, stay off it. But if you want to continue at the same speed or to speed up, then you need to get back on the gas. And, ideally, get back on the gas *as* the clutch comes back up.

So it's clutch up 1...2...gas back on...3.

Now let's tighten that sequence up:

- Accelerate
- Listen to the engine
- Hand down
- Clutch down

MARK JOHNSTON

- Off the gas
- Change gear
- Clutch up: 1...2...
- On the gas
- Clutch fully up...3

Now, remember, changing down is different because you're not generally concerned with the sound of the engine but instead with the speed of the car. Also, you generally change down because you're slowing down, which means you will usually already be off the gas both before and after the gear change.

So, changing down:

- Hand down
- Clutch down
- Change gear
- Clutch up...1...2...3

Which brings us onto...

Using The Gears On Hills

...and one of the skills that many new drivers find tricky to master: **changing down going downhill**.

Now, if you think back to when we were discussing the clutch, the problem in changing down going downhill is *coasting*. Remember, when you press the clutch down going downhill your car will speed up, **unless you brake simultaneously**.

This means you'll need to use the brake to control your speed through the entire gear change.

So, changing **down** going **downhill**:

- Brake gently and **stay on the brake**
- Hand down
- Stay on the brake!

- Clutch down
- Stay on the brake!
- Change gear
- Stay on the brake!
- Clutch up…1…2…3
- Off the brake

Now, this probably sounds quite straightforward but, as I said, this is a skill that does catch a lot of people out because if you lift off the brake at any time before the clutch comes back up then you will speed up. And that will come as a shock to both you and your Supervisor if, say, you're changing down in readiness for a tight turn into a side road!

If your car park has a nice downhill section, then practise this skill. But if it doesn't, this is something that you must practise in a straight line first. **Don't wait until you're actually approaching a downhill junction before trying it for the first time.**

Now the good news…

Changing **down** going **uphill** is much easier because your car will be naturally slowing down throughout the gear change. Much less drama!

That's changing down. Changing **up** going **downhill** is also easy because as you press the clutch down to begin the gear change your car will continue to speed up as it coasts down the hill. In fact, on a steep downhill you don't really need to use the engine in between gears at all. The gradient will effectively do the accelerating for you.

Changing **up** going **uphill** is trickier though. Again, it's down to coasting and the effect the gradient has on the car. So, changing up uphill, you need to drive a little faster, say 10mph faster, than on a level road for each gear change. This extra speed is necessary to carry you through the gear change as the hill will be trying to slow you down.

Gradient, and especially going uphill, also has an effect in our next subject...

Changing Down To Go Faster

Imagine you're going away for a well-earned break, a long weekend. You're going to need to pack, so from the bottom of your wardrobe you drag out your five bags. You have a small rucksack, handy for a day trip, and a monster of a suitcase – one with wheels – that you normally only use for longer holidays. Then there are three other bags, each of which fits somewhere in between those other two. So...which one should you take? Do you want to travel light or go large, or somewhere in between?

Now, your car's engine thinks about its gears in the same way as you're thinking about those bags. The biggest one is great because you can carry the most stuff, but it's heavy. That's like 5th gear. Your engine can pack lots of miles-per-hour but finds it heavy to carry. The small rucksack, though, is like 1st gear. Great for nipping about, easy to carry, for sure, but it can't pack many MPH.

Now, imagine you're arriving at your budget hotel. The lift's broken. Your room's on the fourth floor. And, oh dear, you've brought your biggest bag – the monster with the wheels – the one your engine calls 5th gear. Well, by the time you're halfway up the first flight of stairs you're already wishing that you could swap the monster for one of your smaller bags.

But, when you're *driving* up a steep hill, rather than walking up, you can swap. You can change down into a lower gear. So, rather than having your engine struggling to carry 5th all the way to the top of the hill, you can change down into a lower gear to give your engine a lighter load to carry. You're changing down to go faster.

So, obviously, 3rd gear, or whatever gear you change down into, can't carry as many miles-per-hour as 4th or 5th, but sometimes, if your engine's struggling, give it a smaller load to carry, to help it climb that hill.

Or to help it accelerate…

Imagine catching up with a slow-moving vehicle – a tractor, say, that's doing 25mph – while you're in 4th gear. As you know, your car will just about drive along in 4th at twenty-five. But it won't effectively accelerate, because 4th is just too heavy a load for your engine to carry at such a low speed.

So, to overtake the tractor, rather than lugging 4th gear along, change down into 3rd – to give your engine a lighter load – so that it can accelerate much more quickly.

Which brings us on to the final part of this lesson, the…

Mistakes People Make

The main mistake involves sequence. **Remember: hand down, clutch down.** So, reach down for the gear-stick, think what you're going to do, then clutch down.

But often learners press the clutch pedal down **then** hunt around for the gear-stick, then change gear. This makes the actual gear change much longer than necessary because you're starting the gear change before you've even taken hold of the gear-stick.

But the other problem with falling into the habit of *clutch down, hand down* is that almost everyone who does it eventually ends up looking down at the gear-stick during the gear change. It's like night follows day. Clutch down – look at the gear-stick – hand down! And looking down at the gear-stick as you change gear isn't acceptable on test. You're expected to look where you're going!

53

The other mistake that happens on test is changing gear while turning the steering wheel. The steering has priority. Steer first then change gear. And that includes when you're pulling out of a side road and, as you accelerate, the engine's starting to get a bit noisy. Don't worry about it. A bit of noise for a couple of seconds won't do any harm, even if you can almost feel your Supervisor willing you to change up!

However, it's okay to change gear if you have the steering-wheel turned, say halfway round a roundabout, but you're just holding it still, not turning it. So it's when you're actually turning the wheel that the gear change is going to have to wait for a few more seconds.

So steer then gear. Which is something else to practise before changing up to Lesson 6, where we'll again discuss the clutch then introduce the four essential clutch-control skills that, between them, will give you complete low-speed mastery of your car.

Such a great word: *mastery*!

CONTROLLIN' THE ROLLIN'

Lesson 6

Another lesson for those of you learning in a manual gearbox car.

If you're able to practise this lesson, you'll need a car park or very quiet road, but one with a nice gentle hill. Nothing too steep, but steep enough for you to know that your car will definitely roll when you release the brakes.

Now, if you've followed the lessons through to this point, hopefully you're starting to get a feel for using the clutch and you realise how important it is in helping you control the car. In this lesson, we'll be taking your skills up to the next level, looking at:

- Controlled coasting downhill
- Moving away downhill
- Controlled coasting using momentum
- Holding point control
- The dreaded hill-start
- The angled start

Coasting, as you know, is what happens to a moving car when the clutch is pressed down, the way it rolls along, like a freewheeling bicycle. So, unlike a car's other controls, the clutch doesn't have a direct effect on the car – it doesn't actually make it slow down or speed up – it simply allows it to roll. So, when you're coasting, it's the gradient that's really in control of the car: uphill you'll stop, downhill you'll speed up.

Controlled coasting is using either the car's momentum or the hill's gradient to your advantage. It's a technique only used at speeds below 20mph. On hills, it's using downhill gradients as a *kind of* engine and uphill gradients as a *kind of* brake.

Let's dive in, and start with…

Controlled Coasting Downhill

Picture yourself in busy traffic, facing downhill. The car ahead of you moves forward two-or-three car lengths then stops again. To move up behind it, with your clutch in and in 1st gear, press the **footbrake** – not the gas – and release the handbrake. Then, to move, keep the clutch down but gently ease off the footbrake, until you start to move…

But don't take your foot off the brake completely, because then you'll roll away, faster and faster, like a rollercoaster. The hill will be in control, not you.

So use the footbrake throughout…

Your car's rolling. It's coasting. But you're controlling the rolling with the brake.

This is controlled coasting.

To practise, face downhill, clutch in, 1st gear, with the footbrake on and the handbrake off. Then, keeping the clutch firmly down the entire time, gently ease off the footbrake. **But, remember, not completely off the footbrake.**

Use the footbrake smoothly. Let the car roll a few metres then stop. Stay on the brake. Stay in control. Remember, downhill controlled coasting is *controllin' the rollin'!* So…

Moving Away Downhill

…is easy because your car will simply start to roll forward the moment you release the brakes. In fact, on a steep downhill, you usually don't even need 1st gear, you can use 2nd. After all, 1st gear's really only to get a stationary car moving, so if the hill's going to do that for you, you can just use 2nd.

And you don't need to set the gas either. Again, if the car's going to roll away for you, you don't need to bring the engine into play until the car's moving.

So, moving away downhill goes like this:

- Clutch down
- 2nd gear
- Footbrake on
- Handbrake off…
- Then, release the footbrake
- …and, as you roll down the hill…
- Clutch up…1…2…3

Okay, so that's using a downhill gradient to your advantage. Now let's talk about…

Controlled Coasting Using Momentum

Picture yourself approaching a roundabout on a level road. You look to your right and see one car coming round the roundabout towards you, so you slow down and drop down into 2nd gear. You plan on letting that car to pass then joining the roundabout immediately behind it. But, turns out, that car's going way slower than you'd realised, so you're going to have to slow down even more, down to below 10mph.

Now, with the clutch up, most cars won't go much below 10mph in 2nd gear without complaint. They will shudder and possibly even stall if you try to go any slower than ten with the clutch up. So, as your speed drops down to below ten, you need to press the clutch down...

And now you've got two options:

- **Change down into 1st gear, join the roundabout, then immediately change back up into 2nd**
- **Stay in 2nd and use the momentum of your moving car to use controlled coasting**

The first of these two options will be difficult to do smoothly. You'll likely end up with a shuddering clutch and a noisy engine.

So, let's try option two, then!

It takes a bit of practise, but this technique allows you to stay in 2nd gear, but to drive away again smoothly, even though your speed's dropped down to below 10mph.

To practise controlled coasting using momentum, try this:

- Find a level road
- Drive in 2nd gear at 20mph
- Come off the gas and allow the speed to drop down to 10mph
- Clutch down and let the speed drop to 5mph
- Give the engine a little gas
- Ease the clutch up very gently, feeling the engine pulling you again
- But don't lift the clutch off completely until your speed's back up to 10mph

Essentially, as long as the road's either downhill or level, provided you're still moving, you don't usually need to change back down into 1st gear. You can just stay in 2nd and get moving again quickly and smoothly, even if your speed's down to below

10mph.

So, 1st gear is for when you're stationary or virtually stationary, especially when you're going uphill. Otherwise, 2nd gear will often be smoother. This is a technique you'll be using all the time. You'll be using it when emerging from those junctions where the view of the main road is quite good – *open* junctions – and the road ahead seems to be clear as you approach. It means you'll be going slow enough to stop easily if you need to, but quick enough to slip away in 2nd gear if the road turns out to be clear.

Now let's move onto uphill control…

Let's begin by picturing a little boy, out playing with his football on a hilly street. He wants to kick the ball up the hill to his friend. So he places it down then takes a few steps back to take his run-up. Except, his ball doesn't stay still. No, it rolls down the street after him. To stop the ball from rolling down the hill, then, the boy will either need to hold the ball still, like a **brake**, or use **power** to kick the ball up the hill.

Now, your car works like the football. It naturally wants to roll downhill. So, to stop it rolling away, you're going to need either a brake or engine power, and you're going to need a skill called…

Holding Point Control

We've previously described – in fact, I'm sure you're sick of hearing it – the clutch as working like a tap, controlling the flow of power from the engine to the wheels in the same way as a tap controls the flow of water. So when the clutch pedal is held down the tap is off. No power flows.

Now the biting point, as you know, is the point where the clutch pedal has come up far enough to allow power to drip through to the wheels. We called that Clutch 1. But the holding point is where the clutch is a fraction higher – at Clutch 2 – where the power's trickling through to the wheels.

So, on a level road, at Clutch 2, your car starts moving, but on a steep uphill it doesn't. On a steep uphill it holds still.

To find the holding point, facing uphill, put your car in 1st gear, handbrake on, then ease the clutch up gently, to just above the biting point, to the point where the bonnet lifts up, just a centimetre. Then keep it there for a couple of seconds before pressing the clutch back down again.

That point, where the bonnet's up a centimetre, is the point where the car will hold still if it's facing uphill and you release the handbrake. It won't roll back. But it won't lurch forward either.

So, uphill, at the holding point, even without brakes, the car just holds still.

Oh, but this *lifting the bonnet* lark assumes your car is front-wheel-drive. Most are, especially smaller cars. However, if yours is rear-wheel-drive, as you come up to the holding point your car will squat down at the back. And if yours is four-wheel-drive then it will just kind of feel like it's ready to go!

Anyway – assuming you're front-wheel-drive – to practise, have the car facing uphill, in 1st gear, handbrake on. Then, with a little gas, use the clutch to lift the bonnet up that centimetre and release the handbrake…

Okay, so what did your car do?

- If it rolled back, either the clutch wasn't quite high enough to begin with or else you pressed it back down as you released the handbrake
- If it lurched forward, the clutch was up too high
- But if it stayed still…well done. A round of applause!

To practise further, try this…

Face uphill, 1st gear, handbrake on. Find the holding point and release the handbrake…

This time, with the car holding still, press the clutch down a few centimetres to deliberately let the car roll back a couple of metres… But then – without using the brakes – ease the clutch gently back up again to *catch* yourself as you roll. You'll need to be really smooth with the clutch to do this.

When you practise, ask your Supervisor to keep an eye out for you, to make sure there's nothing behind you. And if, at any time, you find yourself panicking, simply press the clutch down and use the footbrake to stop the car.

As you get the hang of this you can play with the holding point, and you can play with the clutch:

- Squeeze it down to roll back
- Ease it up again to stop
- Clutch a bit higher to creep forward
- Squeeze it back down to find the holding point again

Your goal here is to be able to make the car do what you want without using the brakes. Hold still, roll back, creep forward. Now, this is an essential skill but it takes a lot of practise, and you might not necessarily get the hang of it first-time-out. The good news, though, is that once you have it, this fine control of the clutch – this clutch *finesse*, as the Americans would say – stays with you for life.

But a word of warning… Back in Lesson 3, we described the clutch mechanism, so the bit down in the engine that your clutch pedal controls, as using a friction plate. And things that use friction, including your very expensive clutch, will wear out. Now, practising the above exercise will do your clutch no harm at all, provided you remember two things:

- **To practise for no more than 30 seconds at a time,**

> **then let the clutch *rest* for a couple of minutes by driving normally for a while**
> • **To keep your engine speed no higher than 2,000 RPM**

Rest assured, my driving school car clutches last for 100,000 miles!

Now, on test, one of the things you'll be asked to do is…

The Dreaded Hill Start

The plan here is to move away uphill, without stalling or rolling back. Now, to prevent the engine stalling you're going to need some gas – trying to move away uphill on tick-over just won't work. And to prevent the car from rolling back you're going to need the holding point.

So the hill start procedure is…

- Clutch in
- 1st gear
- Set the gas
- Clutch 1: the bite…
- Then, up a bit higher – to Clutch 2 – the holding point
- Keep your feet still
- Mirror
- Signal
- Blind spot
- Door mirror…
- Then, release the handbrake
- Keep your feet still
- Clutch 3: so all the way up, lifting it gently
- A little more gas to drive away

The final skill we're going to discuss in this lesson is, again, something you'll be asked to do on test. It's called:

The Angled Start

What happens is this: your Examiner asks you to pull over on the left-hand-side of the road, **close** to a parked car. *Close* here means stopping so that you can just see the road surface between you and the other car.

Then, once you have your car secured, your Examiner will simply tell you to **move on when you're ready.**

Now, when you move away, you'll need to keep good clutch control, to keep your car moving slowly, as you steer out quickly to get around the other car, then to straighten up again and drive away. All under control and while watching-out for other traffic.

The other thing to remember here is that, as well as traffic coming up behind you, you'll also need to give-way to traffic approaching from the front.

This is because when you're moving away from a parked position you must give-way to *any* passing traffic. Now, usually that means cars coming up behind you, but here, because you're moving out from behind a parked car, and so because you're going to have to move out onto the *wrong* side of the road, you must also give-way to traffic coming towards you.

So this manoeuvre needs good coordination and good clutch control. It also needs nerves of steel on the part of your Supervisor! So it isn't a good idea to practise this until both of you are sure that your clutch control is up to it!

MARK JOHNSTON

THEORY TEST, SAFETY QUESTIONS ('SHOW ME, TELL ME') & ANCILLARY CONTROLS

Lesson 7

Now, apologies, this is a long lesson with a daunting – but fairly self-explanatory – title, so let's jump right in, and let's start with the…

The Theory Test

It has two parts, the written questions and the *hazard perception* video test, and you must pass both parts at the same time for an overall test pass. So, no, you can't just pass the written questions one week then go back the following week to do the hazard perception.

When you arrive at your local theory test centre, **both parts** of your provisional licence are checked and you're asked to put everything you have with you – bags, mobile phone, whatever – into a locker. And *you* – personally – might also be checked! It's not unusual to be asked to pull up your sleeves so that the test centre staff can check that you haven't written anything on your arms!

Anyway, if you manage to make it past security, head over to your allotted computer terminal and start with the written part of the test. This is done as fifty multiple-choice questions. You're given loads of time, so don't rush...

Take your time.

Various languages are available for the questions, as well as *readers* to help you along, if necessary. If you would like to make use of one of these services, you must book it in advance. Otherwise, it's just assumed that you'll take the test in English and read the questions yourself.

If you get stuck on a question, or you've answered it but would like the chance to look over it again, then you can *flag* individual questions so as to come back to them again at the end of your written questions, before moving onto the hazard perception part of the test. However, it's probably best to make your way through the questions one at a time, answering them all – even if your answer is just an educated guess – and to leave the flag option alone. Lots of folk go back to flagged questions, doubting themselves, and change what turns out to have been a correct answer to a wrong one.

Preparing for your theory is best done using one of the Apps available. A good one will be kept up to date with all the latest questions, will allow you to focus on particular topics, and will keep a record of your practise test scores. So, there's no longer any need to load your desk up with more books than a philosophy student, it'll all be on your phone.

However, there's one book still well worth a careful read: *The Highway Code*. It gives you the rules of the road. Sounds boring, perhaps, but you wouldn't try your hand at a new game or sport without knowing the rules, would you? And investing in a paper copy allows you to make notes in the margins and underline stuff. Proper old school, but it works.

The Highway Code covers pretty much everything you'll need for your theory test and it does it in a short, sharp format. The problem with the Apps is that they essentially just ask questions then tell you whether you were right or wrong. *The Highway Code* gives you the information up front.

For example, did you know that there's a colour-code system of reflectors and cat's eyes used to help you work out what lane you're in when you're driving on a dual carriageway or motorway, at night or in fog? There are at least a dozen questions based on this system that you could be asked in your theory test but, in just one paragraph, *The Highway Code* gives you all the information you'll need to answer those questions.

However, if you don't even know about the colour-code system, let alone how it works, then what's the point of trying to answer questions about it on your App? All that will do is highlight what you *don't* know. So, try to find time to read through *The Highway Code*, along with using a theory App.

Incidentally, one way to remember how the motorway colour-code system works goes like this…

Picture an RAC van – one of those orange breakdown-service vehicles – sitting, first in the queue, at a red traffic light. Okay, so…

An RAC van at a red light.

Now, **RAC**: *Red, Amber, Centre* of the road…

So, the **Red** cat's eyes are on the left-hand-side of, say, a motorway, **Amber** on the right.

Then you have the **Centre** of the road. On a motorway that's the grassy *central reservation*.

Next, think of the traffic light that the RAC van's waiting at. Traffic lights have red, amber and green lights. Red and amber have already been used in our RAC, so that leaves green. Green is the odd one out…

Green is used for slip lanes, side roads and lay-bys.

Finally, our RAC van is first in the queue at the lights, so it's waiting on the white line…

White cat's eyes go along the white lane-lines.

So, a question might be: *you're driving on a three-lane motorway at night. There are white reflectors to your left and right. Which lane are you in?*

Well, as we've seen, the system on a three-lane motorway would be: red to the left, amber to the right, and white along the lane lines. So it'd be:
- Red
- White
- White
- Amber

The answer, then, would be the middle lane, lane two.

Anyway, the point is that *The Highway Code* gives you the chance to work these things out for yourself, rather than just bombarding you with questions.

Now, once you've finished the fifty questions, it's on to the…

Hazard Perception

…part of the test. This is done in **fourteen** one-minute video clips during which you're on the hunt for fifteen hazards. Yep, you've got it – **one of the clips has two hazards**.

Once you begin the hazard perception test you can't pause it.

The clips just keep on coming. So it's finger on the buzzer... Oh, but you don't have to point a cursor at the hazards. You simply click the button.

The main problem people have with this test is in understanding what it's actually about. Firstly, the clue's in the name: *hazard perception*:

  • *Hazard* here is essentially defined as a situation that makes you steer around, slow down, or stop for something
  • *Perception* means to be observant and aware, to look for subtle clues

So this test is not necessarily just hazard *identification*. It's not about waiting until an obvious hazard fills the screen. It's about catching onto those clues that something might be about to happen.

The second thing that catches folk out is thinking they're only allowed to press the button once per clip. That's not the case. You might, on certain clips, press the button perhaps half-a-dozen times.

If you press the button after spotting something – say, a car approaching the end of a side road – you're not penalised if it turns out that the car just stops, where it's supposed to, without any drama. No. You saw the clue. You pressed the button. It's fine. If it turns out to be a false alarm, that's not a problem.

Having said that, if you press the button multiple times in quick succession, like you're playing some sort of rogue special-forces video-game, then you'll be told by the computer that you're cheating, and you won't score any points for that clip.

So, don't go crazy with the button, but don't just sit there with your finger hovering over it, either. Find a balance, somewhere in the middle of the two.

The final thing with hazard perception is with what we'll call the *scoring window*.

So, picture the scene unfolding on the computer screen before you: you're driving along a virtual country road, approaching a bend. Then, just before the bend, you spot a triangular warning sign – miles away, barely visible without binoculars. It's the one with a cow in the middle of it…

A-ha, you think, a potential hazard: cows crossing just around this next bend. So you press the button. And, right enough, your car carries on around the bend… and there's the hazard, an old farmer coaxing a herd of cows across the road. Well done, you!

Except that, at the end of the test, you discover that you scored zero points for that particular clip, because you pressed the button too early!

Now, I realise this doesn't sound fair, but it is possible to be *too* clever. So, the trick is to spot the clue and press the button, but then to count to yourself a steady…1…2…3…and press the button again, just to be on the safe side.

So, the scoring window, for our imagined clip with the cows, started **just** before the sign, not **miles** before it. If you'd pressed the button just before the sign, you would've scored the maximum five points.

Then, from the start of the scoring window, up to the point where you actually see the cows crossing the road, the score counts down, like a rocket about to blast off…5…4…3…2…1!

So, practise those hazard perception clips on your theory test App.

But you can also play…

The Real Life Hazard Perception Challenge!

Okay, so the way this works: as you're being driven somewhere, comfortable in the passenger seat, try literally commentating on what's going on and on what you would do about it. Say it out loud. And try to keep talking. Look well ahead, right up the road, see what's happening. Give yourself plenty to talk about.

Sounds easy, doesn't it? But this is something you'd be asked to do if you ever took an advanced driving test. It gets you thinking, really thinking.

So, warn yourself of the kids messing about at the bus stop, mention the car leaving the petrol station, and congratulate yourself on catching a glimpse of the reflection of *that* bike behind *that* van. Try actually saying what the road signs mean. Say where you think the cars on a roundabout are going to go. Say what gear you'd shift into next.

Then try pointing-out to yourself ten potential dangers in one minute. Try *The Real Life Hazard Perception Challenge.*

Then get whoever's driving to try it…

They're not smiling now, are they?

So, prepare for your theory test, ideally before you even start your driving. It's great, as an instructor, to meet a new pupil and to find out that the theory test has already been done, or at least booked and prepared for.

Now, something else that you can do before you even start your driving is to find your way around the…

Safety Questions ('Show Me, Tell Me') And Ancillary Controls

At the beginning of your driving test, immediately after your Examiner has looked-over your licence and checked your eyesight (by getting you to read a number-plate) you'll be asked to make your way over to your car, where you'll be asked one of your two **Safety Questions**, known as the **show me, tell me** questions.

You're asked one question here – the **tell me** question – in the car park, and the other one – the **show me** question – when you're out on your drive.

Now, although, like in any test, you want to get off to a good start, don't stress over these questions too much because, even if you get both of them completely wrong, you don't fail the test. No, the worst that can happen is that you'll have just one *minor driving fault* scored against you, even if you mess up both questions.

The other thing to remember is that you won't be getting your hands dirty. You don't have to be a mechanic to pass a driving test! These questions take just one or two minutes – that's all – and don't require you to reach for the toolkit.

In this lesson, we're going to be looking at the twenty-or-so questions that have been asked of my pupils over the past few years. But this isn't an exhaustive list. Safety questions come and go. So, the more you know about the basic workings of your car the better: how to open the bonnet, fill it with fuel, use the wipers, and even open the windows!

Which leads us onto the *ancillary* controls...

Your car's ancillary controls are those that you use all the time in everyday driving but aren't actually necessary to make the car move. So, the headlights, for example.

Your use of the ancillary controls is part of the driving aspect of your test and might also relate to one of the safety questions you'll be asked. So, again, the more comfortable you are with these additional controls the better.

So, as in all aspects of your driving, the more you know, and the more you practise, the better you'll get. There's no secret.

In relation to the safety questions and ancillary controls, it's really handy to find someone who can show you around a car and talk you through a few things. Maybe you could even take a few photos of, say, under the bonnet, to help you remember where the bits-n-pieces are.

Anyway, let's now run through our...

Twenty-Or-So Questions

So, there you are, having just met your Examiner, nervously walking over to your car, when your Examiner turns to you and says, *I'd like you to open the bonnet, identify where you'd check the oil, and tell me how to check the oil level.*

Okay – *you've got this!* – start by getting yourself...

Under the Bonnet

First, you need to know how to actually open the bonnet. Three things:

- Pull the lever that unlocks the bonnet from inside the car
- Release the catch under the bonnet itself
- Lift the bonnet up and make sure it stays up

The locking lever inside the car is usually in one of the car's *footwells*, possibly on the driver's side down by the accelerator, or maybe over on the passenger side somewhere. When you find it, give it a gentle pull – it doesn't require any more effort than opening the glove box – and you'll hear a *clunk*. That's the bonnet unlocked.

Now go around to the front of the car...

The lever to actually open the now unlocked bonnet is under the front edge of the bonnet itself. If you feel around under there, you'll usually find it. But, if you can't find it, you might need to squat down – in as dignified a manner as possible – to have a quick look for it and to see how it works.

Finally, heave the bonnet up and make sure it stays up. Some are magic and stay up all on their own, but others need to be propped up by a metal rod which you'll find tucked away in there somewhere.

If you have access to a car, try it a few times – open the bonnet, (if necessary) prop it up, then close it again. Remember, it's all good practise.

Anyway, the bonnet's now safely up, so grab an old cloth and have a quick look around the engine. Your Examiner might ask you to explain how to check and refill any one of the fluids under there. So that's:

- Oil
- Coolant
- Brake fluid
- Windscreen washers

And some cars also have power steering fluid as well. Anyway, if you have someone to help you, get them to run through each of them: how to check them, and if necessary, how to top them up. Use your cloth to wipe things clean and to protect your hands. Oh, and remember to have the engine switched off **before** you open the bonnet and that it's best to do this with a cold engine, not one that's been running recently, as things can get dangerously hot in there.

Anyway, let's run through the list, and start with…

Checking the Oil

To check the engine oil level, so the amount of oil actually in there, you need the engine to be switched off and the car to be parked on a level road. Then locate the dipstick, and also the small round engine-cover that needs to be removed to add more oil. Then:

- Pull the dipstick out of the engine
- Wipe off any oil with your cloth
- Note the measuring marks at the end of the dipstick (you're going to want your oil to be up at the *top* mark, not down at the one nearest the tip)
- Push the dipstick all the way back down into the engine, back from whence it came
- Pull it back out again, keeping it pointing down so that oil doesn't sneak up the dipstick
- Take a look at it
- There's hopefully some oil visible on the dipstick, ideally up at the top mark
- But if there isn't any oil there at all, or if it's down by the mark at the tip of the dipstick, then you need to add some
- It's way easier to add oil than it is to remove it, so only add oil by a *cupful* at a time
- After each cupful, repeat the measuring process until the oil's up at the top mark
- Make sure everything under the bonnet is back where you found it, make sure you've got hold of your cloth, and close the bonnet

Now the coolant:

Coolant is a mixture of water and *antifreeze*. Antifreeze – as its name suggests – is a chemical that prevents the water in there from freezing on a cold winter's night. Now, your engine *burns* fuel so gets really, really hot, and the job of the coolant is to stop your engine from overheating and wrecking itself, so the coolant gets really, really hot as well.

If your car is low on coolant, you can buy it premixed from petrol stations or car accessory shops. Coolant comes in different colours. Don't mix one colour with another – even if one is your *favourite* colour – stick with what's already in your car!

Modern cars have a coolant *header* tank. It's a transparent plastic container – sometimes like a small football, sometimes the shape of a small loaf – with a removable plastic cap on top. The container will be marked to show the *minimum* coolant level. And the cap often comes with a graphic suggesting either that the contents of the container are hot or that you should protect your hand when opening the cap. So, if you do ever intend to open that cap, especially if the engine's been running recently, use your old cloth again, but this time like an oven glove, to protect your hands.

On your safety questions, though, you won't be asked to remove that cap. Just to identify the header tank, tell the Examiner how to check the coolant level, and how to top it up, if necessary.

So, point out the level marking to your Examiner, and mention protecting your hands if you're asked how to add coolant. Next…

Brake Fluid

Brake fluid can also be found in one of those transparent plastic header tanks – this time known as a *reservoir* – but a smaller one. On the reservoir's cap it might say, for example, DOT 4. DOT refers to the type of brake fluid your car uses and, as with the coolant, the types can't be mixed-n-matched.

To check the level of the brake fluid, take a look at the markings on the side of the reservoir to make sure the fluid lines-up between the maximum and minimum marks.

If your Examiner asks you how to add brake fluid, the main detail to stress is that you should try to keep the reservoir and its cap clean. Give them a wipe with that cloth of yours, and place the cap down neatly, making sure it doesn't pick up any bits of muck. Any dirt or grit that gets into the reservoir could lead to dangerous and expensive havoc, so is best avoided!

Now onto the fourth – and easiest – of the under bonnet checks...

The Windscreen Washers

This is another reservoir. This one is usually hidden down below the engine, so all you can see of it is its cap. There's not usually any way of checking the level of the water in the washer reservoir, so you just have to top it up periodically.

Anyway, on test, just point to the cap and mutter something about *putting the windscreen washing water in there.*

Finally, if your car has...

Powered Steering Fluid

...under the bonnet, that'll be in yet another plastic reservoir.

Same as the others, point to the reservoir, point to the level markings, and mention cleanliness if you're asked how to add more fluid.

So that's under the bonnet. Now let's move onto a couple of *tell me* questions that you might be asked about the...

Tyres

There are two: tyre **pressures** and tyre **condition**. As these questions are just *tell me* questions you'll just be standing there, with your Examiner, looking and *sort of* pointing at your tyres, but not actually getting your hands dirty.

Checking tyre **pressures** means seeing that you have just the right amount of air pumped into each tyre. If the pressure's too low then there isn't enough air in there. That could cause your car to not steer or brake as it should, or to use extra fuel, or to quickly wear-out that very expensive tyre of yours.

Checking your tyre air pressures is both one of the most important maintenance tasks you can do and also one of the easiest. So let's get to it…

Four things:

- Check them early in a journey, when the tyres are still cold
- Know how to find out what the tyre pressures should be
- Find a supply of air and a gauge to check them
- Remove, then replace, the valve dust caps

Let's add in some detail.

As you drive, especially if you drive fast, and especially if you drive on a warm day, your tyres heat up. And, as that happens, so the air inside them expands, which increases the pressure of that air in the tyre. To keep your checks accurate, the recommended tyre pressures for your car are based on cool tyres, tyres that haven't been driven on today for any more than a few miles. So, if you have to drive to a petrol station to check your tyre pressures, make it your local one.

The correct air pressure for your tyres can be found online or in your car's handbook. But most cars also have a sticker on them, with a chart showing those recommended pressures. To find the sticker, start by opening the driver's door and looking around there. If it's not there, try under the bonnet.

On test, you don't need to know the actual tyre pressures for your car, you just need to be able to tell your Examiner how to find them. So, find the tyre pressure sticker for your car so that you can point it out, or, failing that, just mutter something about Google.

Notice that there's probably a difference in recommended tyre pressures between front and back, and also between when you're driving on your own and when your car's loaded-up with luggage and passengers. There might also be a different pressure shown for motorway driving. And these figures are shown as both PSI – pounds-per-square-inch – and Bar – the metric system. Use whichever you prefer.

Then you need to find yourself a tyre pressure gauge and some air. Maybe you have a foot-pump or even an air compressor at home, or maybe you need to use the compressor at the petrol station. That's over where it says *air*, which is usually where there's also a water tap that you can use.

Anyway, if you're at the petrol station, park over where it says *air*. See if it's free or coin operated. Then whip off the dust caps from all four tyres...and keep them safe. If it's a digital system, set the figure for your car on the machine. Then fit the air valve snugly over your tyre's valve. The machine will make all kinds of hissing noises, then beep when it's finished. Finally, when you're all done, replace the dust caps.

Another question your Examiner might ask is: ***how do you check that your tyres are in good condition?***

This comes down to two parts of the tyre: the ***sidewall*** and the ***tread…***

The ***sidewall's*** the bit that has the writing on it – *Goodyear*, or whatever. You're looking for obvious signs of damage: **cuts or bulges**.

Imagine scraping your hand on a wall and having a sliver of skin that you can lift up, or burning yourself with an iron, giving yourself a blister. That's the kind of thing you're looking for: a cut or a bulge. Damage to the sidewall can't be repaired. The tyre is now dangerous so should be replaced.

Once you've finished with the sidewall, check the *tread*...

The tread's the part of the tyre that comes into contact with the road. Those grooves around the tyre must be at least **1.6mm** deep. They're there to pump water from a wet road away from under your tyre. They're super important. To check them, you could call into a tyre garage and ask them to do it for you, or you could do it yourself, either with a *tread depth gauge*, or by running your fingernail around inside the grooves, feeling for the bumps that you'll find every few inches.

Those bumps are called ***wear bars***, and they're roughly 1.6mm up from the bottom of the groove. So, as the rubber wears ***down***, the wear bars kind of rise ***up***, until, when they reach the top of the groove, flush with the main part of tyre itself, that tyre's worn out.

So, that's the engine and tyres looked over. Now let's check...

The Electrics

Start with an easy one. Your Examiner says, ***show me how you'd check that the horn's working.***

So, where's the hooter – the horn – on your car? Go on then...you know you want to! *Beep beep*!

Next...let there be light! The first position on the light switch, sometimes known as your ***sidelights***, puts on your tail lights and your low-powered front lights. But the sidelights are also – and more correctly – known as the ***parking-lights*** because this light setting is really only for when you're stationary, so, for example, parked on an unlit country road or pulled over on a city street.

Note that some modern cars have fairly bright front lights – known as ***daytime running lights*** – that are on all the time while you're driving, and that these lights actually **dim down** – they're less bright – when you switch on your parking lights. So the old-fashioned idea of driving around with just the *sidelights* on definitely doesn't work for modern cars.

Or any cars, for that matter, because when you're driving, and you want your lights on, you should use **dipped** headlights…

Dipped is the second position on your light switch. You'll probably see a green light come on, on the dashboard. Dipped means they're focussed down and to the left, so as not to **dazzle** oncoming drivers, to not temporarily blind them.

So, use your dipped beam when you're driving, not just sidelights. Remember, sidelights are just parking lights. So use dipped headlights when you're driving at night or in **poor visibility**. Poor visibility means, even though *you* can see just fine, it may be harder than usual for other people to see you. So in heavy rain, say, or at dusk, use dipped headlights.

The next stage on your car's lights is **full beam**, also known as **main beam**. Full beam is brighter than dipped, and the focus of the light is thrown further forward and straight ahead, rather than down and to the left. When your lights are on full beam you get a blue warning light.

Only use full beam on unlit roads when it won't dazzle anyone. So, if there's anyone ahead of you, either travelling towards you or going in the same direction as you, or even waiting to emerge from a side road, just use dipped beam.

You can only switch to full beam if your dipped headlights are already on, but, even if your headlights are off, you can still **flash** the headlights – that's a quick burst of full beam. This is generally done by pulling the indicator switch back towards you.

Now, officially – so that means, according to *The Highway Code* – the headlight flasher's only function is to warn other drivers that you're there. So it's a visible, rather than audible, version of your horn.

But, be wary of cars flashing their lights at you, and don't take it for granted that you know what the flash means. Communication breakdowns happen because different drivers use their headlight flasher to mean different things. Some are telling you to get out of their way, some are telling you that they're going to let you go ahead of them, some are warning you of a hazard ahead, while yet others are just saying *hello*!

Now, on your driving test, if you're absolutely certain that another driver's headlight flash is meant for you, and you're absolutely certain what that other driver means by it, then you can act on it, you don't have to just sit there. But you must be **absolutely** certain.

However, on test, you're absolutely not allowed to flash your lights at anyone else – unless, that is, you're using *The Highway Code's* definition of what the headlight flasher is for, in other words, you're warning someone that you're there.

Your car will also have *fog lights* – either one or two at the back, and possibly two at the front. And, on your dash, you'll have warning lights to let you know when the fog lights are on.

So when should you use your fog lights? Er...when it's foggy! Well, *The Highway Code* says when visibility is down to less than one hundred metres. But, seriously, what does one hundred metre visibility really look like? I have no idea! So, when it's foggy – although not the official wording – kind of makes sense.

Anyway, the front fog lights are not there to make your car look like a rally car, and the rear ones are not there to make your car more visible in the rain. They're for when it's foggy.

Using your front fog lights when it isn't foggy will potentially dazzle other drivers because the light is bright but not focused down and to the left. So, unlike your dipped headlights, front fog lights are just bright splashes of light.

And using your rear fog lights when it isn't foggy can also be dangerous. The traffic following you might not be able to see your brake lights clearly because of the brightness of your fog lights, especially if the design of your tail lights places your brake lights and fog lights close together. And again, same as the front, only use your rear fog lights when it's foggy – so, again, visibility down to less than one hundred metres.

Next, the washers and wipers. For the wipers to work, if your engine's switched off, you'll need the car's electrics to be switched on. This is sometimes known as *ignition*. It's when the key is turned part way, far enough around to power-up the dashboard warning lights. On a key-card system, for *ignition*, you might need to put the ***key-card*** in the ***reader***, that's the slot the key-card goes into.

For your windscreen wipers, the first click on the switch will either be for an automatic system, which senses when rain's falling on your windscreen, or ***intermittent*** – when the wipers swish every few seconds. The second click of the switch has the wipers wiping steadily across the windscreen. And the third click has your car thinking it's a lifeboat, the wipers now going top speed!

If your Examiner asks you to wash the screen, generally you'd pull the wiper switch back towards you and hold it for a few seconds. This will fire a jet of water at the windscreen as the wipers swish backwards and forwards.

Finally, there's the rear-window washer and wiper. On some cars, if you have the wipers on, the rear wiper will come on automatically when you shift into reverse gear.

*

Now, let's move onto the heating system, because the other occasion when you'll find yourself needing to clear your windows is when they steam-up, which often happens on rainy days.

If at all possible, avoid wiping steamed-up windows with your bare hands. Yes, smearing the condensation around may give you a temporary improvement, but it will only be temporary, and it'll soon dry to a smudgy mess. It's far better to use your *demisters* instead.

The demisters work by blasting warm air up onto the windscreen, rather than down onto your feet. Using this in conjunction with your heated rear window and, if your car has one, the electrically heated windscreen, will soon sort things out. Learn how to use these controls whilst driving, as you might be asked to do just that on test.

Now, when you first start the engine, an array of coloured warning lights illuminates the dashboard for a couple of seconds before they – *hopefully* – go out. Hopefully because if one of the warning lights stays on, or comes on when you're driving, it spells trouble. Just how much trouble is defined by the colour: an amber light is bad, a red light is really bad.

Switch your electrics on and off a few times to get to know your way around these warning lights.

On test you might be asked to check a particular system by switching the electrics *on* and simply confirming that the warning light has gone *off*. Pretty basic stuff, but only if you know where the warning lights are!

There are another four things that you could be asked about that you can do from the comfort of the driver's seat:

- Footbrake
- Handbrake
- Powered steering
- Head-restraints

You can check the basic function of the brakes by simply

pressing down on the brake pedal or pulling up on the handbrake lever. You should feel resistance from both. So, if the footbrake flops to the floor, or the handbrake lever comes up to your armpit, you have a problem.

Your car's powered steering is powered by the engine. When the engine's running, the steering-wheel should turn easily. If it doesn't, if it feels the same as it does when the engine's switched off, then the powered steering isn't working.

And finally, your car's **head-restraints**, or **headrests**, should line up with the centre of your head, so with your ears. If they don't, they can be adjusted by pressing in the button where the metal rods from the head-restraint go into the seat, then moving the headrest itself either up or down.

*

So, as we said at the start of this lesson, try to get someone to show you around a car to take a look at the things we've discussed here. And if you have your own car, get yourself familiar with it to the point where you're comfortable tackling all of the various things we've talked about. The better you are at this stuff, the better you'll be at the Safety Questions and also the better you'll look during the actual driving if, say, it chucks it down with rain but you're able to calmly switch on your wipers and headlights!

The more you practise, the better you'll get.

And, with that, we come to the end of Section 1. Hopefully you now feel that you either have *mastery* of your car or else – if you haven't been able to practise just yet – a good understanding of the theory of car control.

In Section 2, we'll move on to the rules of the road and traffic situations, and we'll begin, in Lesson 8, by looking at a crucial aspect of driving and passing a driving test, known to Driving Instructors as *MSM*…

MARK JOHNSTON

MIRROR, SIGNAL, MANOEUVRE

Lesson 8

In *The Highway Code* – that I'm sure you've now read from cover-to-cover – you'll see the initials MSM used. It stands for:

- Mirror
- Signal
- Manoeuvre

Let's start with the...

Mirrors

Mirror, signal, manoeuvre...it's the system your Examiner expects you to use. Your name might be Lewis Hamilton, but if you don't use the mirror, signal, manoeuvre routine, you don't pass.

By the way, when we say ***manoeuvre*** in this context we're talking about a situation where you'll need to change your speed or change your ***course***. And change your course essentially means steering, so for a junction or a lane change or a parked car.

On your test, whatever situation you find yourself having to deal with, you must start by looking in your mirror. The system is mirror then signal then manoeuvre.

Mirror first. Then one of the three S's...

So it's mirror BEFORE you:

- **Signal**
- **Steer**
- **Speed**

So, if your Examiner says, *at the end of the road, turn left*, they will expect you to look in your mirror *before* you either signal or start slowing down for the junction. And when they see a parked car up ahead, they'll watch closely to see that you check your mirror *before* you move out to pass that car. And if they see a green light up ahead, they'll watch both you and the lights to see that – if the lights change – you use your mirror *before* you brake.

I bet you know of someone who's failed their test *on mirrors* but were complaining, saying that they'd used their mirrors *loads.* Well, maybe they did, but if those mirror checks came either after, or simultaneously with, popping an indicator on, then their Examiner will still have marked a fault against them. It must be mirror *before...*

Mirrors, then, are a big deal on your test. Failing to use them correctly is one of the main reasons for...er...failing.

And remember that your car has *mirrors* – plural, more than one. As well as your rear-view mirror you also have door mirrors.

And then there are your blind-spots to consider as well...

Blind-spot checks are for when you're moving away or lane changing, including the lane change you'll generally need to do when exiting a roundabout after turning right.

Make blind spot checks according to your direction of travel. So, if you're moving away from the left-hand kerb, check your right-hand blind-spot.

A **blind-spot check before moving away** is a final look round to check for traffic emerging from any side-roads or driveways that aren't visible in your door mirror. So you'll need to **turn your shoulders** slightly to look round towards your car's *'B' Pillar* – that's the vertical piece of metal that your door closes against, the bit helping to hold your roof up.

But a **blind-spot check on the move** – for a lane change – is just the quickest of glances to look *along* **your shoulder**, turning your head through ninety degrees. Literally one second. That's it.

It would be potentially dangerous to spend any longer than that looking behind you, rather than where you're actually going. And remember, the blind-spot is right *there*, just over your shoulder. Don't try to spin round in your seat or look back along the road behind you – you have mirrors for that!

Okay, so all of these – the rear-view mirror, the door mirrors and the blind-spot checks – fall into your mirror, signal, manoeuvre routine.

So, if you're, say, changing lanes from left to right, it's:

- Rear-view mirror
- Right door-mirror
- Indicate right
- Right blind-spot glance
- Back to the right door-mirror
- All clear?
- Change lanes

When changing lanes, if it's busy, you might have to check your door mirror several times, looking for a gap to move into. And if a big vehicle's passing you, glance into the blind-spot as it passes, in case another – smaller – vehicle is following closely behind it.

Okay. What else? Approaching a red traffic light when you're turning left would be something like:

- Rear-view mirror
- Left door mirror
- Indicate left
- Brake and stop
- Then when the lights change and you move away
- Left door-mirror again, for cyclists
- Left blind-spot glance
- Turn left

And finally, turning right into a side road:

- Rear-view mirror
- Right door-mirror
- Indicate right
- If possible, position over to the right
- Another door-mirror check, for, say, motorbikes
- Turn right

So that's the system used by your Examiner to mark your use of the mirrors on test.

But there's more…

If it was only necessary to use your mirrors before you signalled, or whatever, then it could theoretically be possible to drive for an hour up a motorway and not bother with your mirrors at all. But the key to using your mirrors correctly is to *always* know what's going on around you. So, *at all times*, as an Examiner might say; not just for the couple of seconds before you make a particular manoeuvre.

The Highway Code suggests using your mirrors *frequently*. This is good advice. So, on your test, the idea is to merge both of these mirror techniques together: to use your mirrors both *before* and *frequently*.

During your first few lessons, if you drove in heavy traffic, your

Supervisor could happily take the mirrors off the car and you wouldn't even notice. You'd be far too busy watching where you're going to worry about much else.

But an experienced driver, in that same heavy traffic, would be a nervous wreck unless their mirrors were adjusted perfectly, just how they like 'em. The experienced driver, then, likes to be aware of the *big picture*.

Picture yourself driving into work on a fairly busy road – two lanes going in the same direction, driving along at 30mph – when, suddenly, the car ahead of you hits the brakes...

Now, if you're aware of the *big picture*, so if you're aware of, say, the van in the lane alongside you, you will brake hard and stay in a straight line. You will instinctively know not to swerve into the other lane. But if you haven't been using your mirrors frequently, so you haven't seen the van, you might assume that the lane alongside you is clear. You might swerve.

So if you're suddenly forced into action and *then* you look in your mirrors it's already too late. But if you use your mirrors frequently, keeping yourself updated on the traffic behind and alongside you, you will always be aware of that *big picture*.

Okay, so let's assume you're now using your mirrors correctly, you know what's going on around you. Now, how are you going to let other people know what you're going to do next? How are you going to communicate? Well, indicators are the main way drivers communicate with other folk, the main way they...

Signal

...what they're planning on doing next. **An *indicator* is just one type of *signal*** – a flashing orange light. But a signal can be as subtle as a nod of the head. Your brake lights are a signal. Your reversing light is a signal. And your position in the road is a signal.

If you're positioned properly, say, waiting to make a right turn, but you're indicating *left*, other drivers will still know you're turning right. They'll just assume you've got the wrong indicator on! Your position in the road *signals* where you're going, even more so than your indicator does.

That's one of the things that can be confusing for us when we watch a lorry turning. A lorry driver will often position their vehicle differently from the cars around them. They might need to swing out to take a wide turn at a roundabout or a side road, often using the *wrong* side of the road.

And talking of confusing… *Not* indicating is just as much a signal as actually indicating. I mean, how many junctions do you pass straight through on your morning commute? How many junctions where you *signal* that you're continuing along the main road by *not indicating*?

That's the reason people get so annoyed by drivers who don't indicate at junctions. Because, by **not** indicating, they're actively telling other people that they're **not** turning…

So, if you don't INDICATE before you turn at a junction, you're SIGNALLING that you're going straight on.

But if an indicator is a signal to others, and if there's definitely nobody else about, then surely there's no need to indicate? It'd be like waving goodbye to a friend after they'd already closed their front door! Completely pointless.

However, on a driving test, there is an argument for indicating anyway, even if there's clearly nobody else around, *just in case*. After all, your Examiner won't fault you for indicating when you're moving away or when you're at a junction just because there's nobody else about. I mean, where's the harm? But they **will** fault you if you choose not to indicate but then somebody catches you out by turning up unexpectedly.

It's up to you. If you're moving away, pulling over, or dealing with a junction, and you're absolutely certain that nobody will benefit from you using an indicator, then it's okay to choose not to. But, if I were you, I'd indicate anyway. Just in case.

In town, often people will benefit from your indicator even if you're in a lane that's only for traffic going in one particular direction…

Say you're approaching a set of traffic lights, a set where there's a lane marked with a nice big arrow – a lane that's just for turning left. So you might think there's not much point indicating. I mean, if you're in that lane, surely everyone knows you're turning left?

Well, not necessarily. All the local drivers should know, but what about strangers just passing through? If you're stationary, waiting for the lights to change, maybe your car's the one covering the arrow, hiding it from those other drivers. And what about the pedestrians, standing there, waiting for the green man to come on? Do they know the lane you're in is left-turn-only? Who knows? So stick one on. Just in case.

When using your indicators, timing when to put them on – and switch them off again, for that matter – is an important factor. Say you're moving away from the side of the road, or changing lanes on a busy dual-carriageway, it's important that you don't shock other drivers by sticking your indicator on just as they're about to pass you. They'll think you haven't seen them, that you're going to pull out. You'll scare the life out of them.

Sometimes you need to turn your indicators off to *break* a signal. Say you need to change lanes in order to turn at a junction that's still a fair way off. Indicate once for the lane change – **break the signal for a few seconds** – then indicate again, as you get closer to the junction. That way, following traffic doesn't think you've changed lanes then just accidentally kept your indicator on. **They see two distinct signals: one for the lane change, one for the junction.**

At a junction, when you're coming up to the end of a road, the driver following you knows that you've got to slow down, and knows that you've got to turn one way or the other, so there's no point in you indicating from miles away. A few car lengths from the junction will do just fine.

But, on the other hand, if you're approaching your turn-off on a fast main road, it's good to get your indicator on nice-n-early, early enough to warn following traffic that you're about to begin *slowing down* for the junction. It can be really annoying, when you're following someone in that situation, to have their brake lights suddenly flash on – forcing you to brake – only for them to *then* indicate.

Indicator timing is a balancing act. You want to make sure people know what you're planning on doing in good time, but you're also trying not to indicate so early that you might mislead them.

On test, if you're asked to *take the next road on the right*, but there's a petrol station between you and that road, wait until you've passed the petrol station before indicating right for the turn. If you're asked to take the next road on the left, but there's a car parked just before the turn, wait until you're out – positioned to pass the parked car – before indicating left. **Don't indicate *left* but then move out to the *right*.**

After a junction, generally the indicators will turn themselves off. It's called *self cancelling*. So when you straighten up it isn't usually necessary to switch them off. But sometimes it is. Sometimes they don't go off, especially after moving away or changing lanes. Then it's important for you to realise your indicators are still on, and to turn them off yourself. They're really misleading if you leave them on, and the last thing you want is for your Examiner to have to tell you to turn an indicator off.

Oh, and click your indicators on and off, nice and gently, with your fingertips. Try to avoid letting go of the steering-wheel. There's no need and, again, you could be marked-down on test if it affects your steering.

Only give signals that tell other people what *you're* going to do. Don't give any signals to tell other people what you'd like *them* to do. So don't wave other traffic past you, when you're in the middle of a reversing manoeuvre. If they decide to pass, that's up to them, not up to you.

That includes using your headlight flasher or your car's horn. Remember, they're just there to warn other people of your presence, if you think they haven't seen you yet. They're not there for you to tell them to go, or to wait, or whatever.

Having said that, if somebody else signals to you in some way – say they wave to let you out of a side road – it's okay for you to go, provided you're sure that it is *you* they're signalling to, and that you're sure you know what it is they mean. So, if a car zooming towards you does a quick flash of its headlights, what does that really mean? Perhaps you'd *like* it to mean they're going to slow down and let you out. But does it? Who knows? So it might be safest to wait and make sure.

Finally, let's give a special mention to the right indicator. It has three jobs. It can tell folk that you're **moving away** from the left side of the road, or that you're **turning right**, or that you're **moving to the right**.

The phrase *moving to the right* includes passing parked cars and other types of overtaking, including overtaking pedestrians or cyclists.

If you're forced to stop behind a parked car, to wait for oncoming traffic to pass, wait with your right indicator on. It tells drivers behind you, as well as oncoming vehicles, that you haven't just parked badly but that you're waiting for a gap in traffic. Most drivers won't overtake a car that's indicating right.

And you should also indicate right when you're passing vehicles parked on a fast road – a main road or a country lane – because it's comparatively rare to find parked cars there, so following drivers might be caught out by you moving out to the right.

But if you're driving in a built-up area there could be literally hundreds of cars parked about the place – they're everywhere – so you can't indicate past them all, you'd never have your right indicator off! I mean, what if there's a whole line of parked cars, followed by a right turn that you plan to take? How can any following traffic be expected to realise that you're planning on taking that turn if you've had your indicator on for the entire length of the street?

So, use your right indicator to tell folk you're *moving to the right*, including when:

- Moving away from the left kerb
- Turning right
- Overtaking pedestrians or cyclists
- Waiting behind a parked vehicle for a gap in oncoming traffic
- Passing parked vehicles on a fast or country road

But it's NOT usually necessary to indicate right before passing parked cars in 30mph limits – although, of course, you must first use your mirrors!

JUNCTION BASICS

Lesson 9

As the title suggests, once you've read through this lesson, if you're then able to practise, get your Supervisor to drive you over to a suitable area, a quiet housing estate or a leafy suburb, and have a drive. But then, once you've driven successfully for an hour-or-so, get your Supervisor to drive you home again. Don't be thinking you're ready for any busy traffic on the drive home. Get a few hours under your belt around these quiet roads first, giving yourself loads of time to get comfortable controlling your car, before you have to start worrying too much about traffic and what other drivers are doing.

So, before you move onto those more *serious* roads, in these quiet areas you should be able to start, stop and steer accurately, and be able to creep forward at junctions with your car under control – including both uphill and downhill junctions.

And you also need to know what's going on, to understand how the junctions you meet work, so who has priority and why, and in what sequence traffic should move through those junctions.

The aim here is for your Supervisor to be able to relax, to be able to simply direct you to turn left and turn right, without having to give you basic instructions – you know, to brake or to change gear or to, ***mind that *&%$ing car!***

But, if you're not yet able to practise actual driving, when you're out-n-about take a series of photos and short videos of the junctions around your local area. Take these photos from each of the directions and roads approaching the junctions. Make sure to include any signs and painted lines. Then take a few minutes to just watch the junction, especially if you don't have any road experience to speak of, to watch the sequence that the traffic moves away in, to see who waits for who.

Okay, so in this lesson we'll discuss:

- Priority
- Priority at junctions
- Crossing the path of oncoming traffic
- Crossroads
- White lines
- Road signs
- The General Rule
- Clearance from stationary vehicles
- Meeting other traffic
- Pedestrians at junctions
- Basic left and right turns

Let's begin with dealing with traffic situations and…

Priority

This is the number one reason for driving test fails. So, if you're sitting comfortably…

As you approach any traffic situation, the first thing you'll need to work out is who has **right of way** – so who has **priority**. In other words, who goes first.

At traffic lights, for example, the guys with the green light have priority – they can go – while the guys on red must stop at the line and wait. Traffic lights, then, alternate priority.

On roundabouts, priority goes to the guys already on the roundabout. So it's the traffic joining the roundabout that waits. But that doesn't necessarily mean the guys joining the

TEACH YOURSELF TO DRIVE IN 20 LESSONS

roundabout have to *stop*. No, they might be able to keep moving, but they must **give-way** to the traffic already on the roundabout...

To *give-way* way means to not inconvenience the traffic that has priority in the situation you're dealing with. It means not forcing that traffic to either have to steer round you or have to slow down for you.

But, again, a situation where you must give-way doesn't necessarily mean that you must stop...

So, the best way of dealing with a give-way situation is to drive slowly enough to be safe – so that you can stop easily, if necessary – but to keep going if the way's clear.

This is known as **safe progress**.

So, approach give-way situations thinking, *I'll probably have to stop here, but I'll hopefully be able to keep going.*

So, who has...

Priority At Junctions

Picture a T-junction on a normal two-way road in a nice quiet area – it's a junction with the usual lines painted on it – and imagine yourself facing the junction, so that the road you're on ends at the road ahead of you, at the 'T' of the junction.

Now, the road you're facing, so the one that continues through the junction – from left to right, ahead of you – is called the **major road**, and the one you're on – because it ends at the junction – is called the **minor road**. A junction can only have one major road but it can have two-or-more minor roads.

Pulling out from the minor road onto the major road is called *emerging*. And when you're emerging you must try not to force anyone driving along the major road to slow down for you. You must give-way. **The major road has priority.**

99

So the first question to ask yourself as you approach a junction is: **who's on the major road?** And if it's not you, if you're on the minor road, then you must give-way to the traffic that *is* on the major road.

The second question that you need to ask yourself is: **who's turning right?**

Okay, back to our junction. So there's the major road, with cars driving along the road, coming from both your left and right…

Now, picture one of the drivers, coming from your left – along the major road – who's indicating right. So, this guy wants to turn right into the minor road, towards you. This guy, then, needs to…

Cross The Path Of Oncoming Traffic

So this guy must give-way to the oncoming traffic – so to stop, if necessary – before starting the turn and crossing their path. So, same idea, that guy mustn't inconvenience the oncoming traffic.

So, question 2 was to ask: who's turning right? And if the answer is that you are, then you must give-way to oncoming traffic before you turn across in front of them.

So, in summary: at our T-junction the traffic moves through the junction in the following sequence:

- Priority 1 is the car on the major road that is continuing through the junction, so that's the car coming from your right
- Priority 2 is the one on the major road, the guy coming from your left, who's turning right into the minor road towards you
- Priority 3 is you, waiting on the minor road for the major road to clear

So that's priority at a T-junction. But what if it's a...

Crossroads

That's a major road joined by **two** minor roads that are opposite one-another.

So, imagine a busy crossroads with two cars coming towards each other – both on the major road – both indicating right. Now what happens?

Well, we know that because these two cars are on the major road they have priority over traffic on the minor roads. That much is clear. But here, **both** cars are on the major road and both are turning right, so that complicates things because neither of them has priority over the other.

And to complicate things even further, there are two ways they can sort this out:

- 1:Pass around behind each other – this is called passing *right side-to-right side*
- 2: Pass in front of each other – *left-to-left*.

Now, of the two ways of turning right at a crossroads, right-to-right is only done very rarely. Usually cars pass in front of each other, left-to-left.

Nowadays, most crossroads are controlled by traffic lights. So, the next time you're out-n-about, watch how the cars turn right at a traffic light junction. See where they stop to give-way to oncoming traffic, and watch whether they pass in front of each other or behind each other. Do they go left-to-left or right-to-right?

*

Now, sometimes junctions are unmarked, so there aren't any

lines painted on the road surface…

In that case, at a T-junction, the road that clearly **ends** at the junction is generally considered to be the minor road.

But, at a crossroads it's trickier, because there's no obvious end, no obvious major road, so no obvious priority. Everybody – traffic on each of the four roads – is expected to work together to get through the junction safely.

But, having said that, most junctions do have…

White Lines

Let's get back to our imaginary T-junction, and take a look at the lines painted there…

First, there's the *hazard line*. That's the one running up the centre of one-or-both of the roads at the junction. It's a long, broken line, with short gaps between the lines. It's there, firstly, to clearly mark-out the two sides of the road. And, secondly, a hazard line is used – funnily enough – to warn you of a hazardous area…

Here the hazard is the junction. In town it might be a bus stop or a pedestrian crossing. Out in the countryside it might be a side road or a bend. Anyway, lines along the centre of the road work on the principal of: *the more paint, the more hazard*.

So, on, say, a dual carriageway or a one-way street, where all the traffic's moving along in the same direction, you'll find *lane lines*. These are short white lines separated by long gaps. There's very little paint being used here because these are considered to be the safest type of roads.

In two-way traffic the line up the middle of the road is called the *centre line*. It looks similar to the lane line, but has ever-so-slightly longer lines and ever-so-slightly shorter gaps because two-way traffic is ever-so-slightly more hazardous than one-way traffic.

Sometimes along the centre of the road you'll see a **hatched** area – that's a series of diagonal lines used to keep traffic apart. Hatching can be used to protect traffic that's using a lane which is only for turning either left or right. Or it can be used to make the road *seem* narrower than it really is – like some kind of optical illusion – to help keep drivers focused on their lane.

Clipping across the end of a hatched area to reach a new lane is okay, but generally you should avoid casually driving across those hatched areas, unless you're forced out by, say, a row of parked cars.

On fast, open roads, you will often see **continuous white lines** along the centre of the road. These are used for the most hazardous parts of our roads, so crests of hills, blind bends, that kind of thing. Essentially, if the line nearest to you is a continuous – known as a *solid* – white line you're in a no-overtaking area. You're not allowed to cross a solid line, except in an emergency.

*

Okay, so that's the lines that go *along* the road. Now let's go back to our T-junction and talk about the lines that go *across* the road at the junction, the ones separating the minor road from the major road.

The line going from the right of the hazard line over to the right-hand kerb is the *carriageway line*. It's a single, short, dotted line, and it's there to show the traffic on the major road where the major road's going. It's like a continuation of the major road's kerb, done in white paint.

Finally, the line going from the left of the hazard line over to the left-hand kerb is the *give-way line*. It's a double broken white line, and it tells the minor road traffic that they've reached the end of the road. It's saying that the road you're on is now the minor road at this junction, so the traffic on the road ahead of you has priority.

In your junction photo gallery, try to get images of all of the road markings we've mentioned here.

White lines, then, are one of the ways that the road communicates with you. The other way is through the use of...

Road Signs

At most T-junctions, like the one we've been imagining up to now, there aren't any signs, just the lines painted on the road. So, as we've discussed, that's the **hazard line**, the **carriageway line** and the **give-way line**.

But, at about **one give-way junction in a hundred**, you'll also see a road sign alongside the junction in the shape of an **upside-down**, or *inverted*, **triangle**. And, as well as the sign, you'll also see an inverted triangle painted on the road, immediately before the give-way line.

The inverted triangle is the *end of the road sign*, used here to warn you that the junction you're approaching is especially dangerous in some way. It warns you to take extra care.

Notice that the inverted triangle sign also has the words *Give Way* on it. That's because you're now at the actual junction. But any inverted triangle signs you saw on the approach to the junction were blank in the middle – these were warning you that there was a junction coming up.

So, those extra markings, then, are at about one junction in a hundred...

But on **one junction in a thousand**, you'll see a *stop sign*. These are octagons, eight sided, and they're painted bright red, with *stop* in white. The stop sign is used in conjunction with a ***stop line*** – that's a thick, solid white line, painted in place of the more common give-way line.

When you reach a stop line you must stop! And that's actually stop. Not just slow right down. Sounds obvious, I know, but if you don't stop, and a policeman sees you, it could be penalty points. And on test, if you fail to stop at a stop line…yep…it'll be a fail.

So, because both the end of road sign and the stop sign are considered to be super important, they each get their own dedicated shape: the inverted triangle and the octagon. But most other signs fall into one of three *family* shapes…

Circles give orders. Think of the letter 'O' in *order*. Red circles tell you things that you must not do. Blue circles tell you things that you must do.

Triangles give warnings. Take a look at the button or switch for your car's hazard warning lights and you'll usually see a little triangular graphic there.

Rectangles give information. Think of the shape of a text book or a computer screen.

So, to recap:

- Triangles warn
- Rectangles inform
- Circles order
- **Red** circles say ***don't***
- **Blue** circles say ***do***

Armed with this knowledge of shape and colour, you don't then need to learn every single sign in *The Highway Code* because you can *read* the traffic signs. You can work-out what they mean by literally describing the little graphic shown in the middle of the sign…

A triangle with a bicycle in the middle says **warning of bicycles**. And a red circle with a bicycle in the middle, says **don't cycle here**. But a blue circle with that same bike in it says, **do cycle – it's a cycle path**.

So signs work to a system of rules. And so do traffic lanes. Knowing how the road works, including positioning the car and using lanes correctly, can be a real frustration for new drivers because it's something that experienced drivers seem to just instinctively *get*. But fear not, because there's a simple way of understanding what's going on, and it's known as…

The General Rule

Which sounds very grand, doesn't it? *The General Rule*. But it's not. The general rule simply says that we should, **drive on the left, unless turning right or overtaking**.

Well, usually! Say at 99% of junctions, anyway. The other 1% has a mixture of road signs and painted arrows to tell us that *at this particular junction* we should ignore the General Rule and do what those signs and arrows are telling us to do instead.

So, at some junctions, the left-hand lane might be left turn only, while the right-hand lane is marked with a straight-ahead arrow. Now, on test, if you're supposed to be going straight on at this junction, your Examiner won't point-out to you that it's the right-hand lane that's arrowed for straight-ahead. You're expected to take note of the arrows and make any necessary lane changes yourself.

The other occasion when we stray from the General Rule is when joining a one-way street or a one-way system. Then, if there's a choice of lanes, simply join the one-way street in the lane nearest to where you're joining from, even if it's the right-hand lane. Then stay in that lane, unless it's blocked by, say, a parked vehicle, in which case you'll need to change lanes **twice**: once to pass the parked vehicle, then a second time to get back into the lane you originally came from…

And all without any instruction from your Examiner, it's all down to you.

However, if your Examiner wants you to move into another lane *permanently*, then they'll ask you to change lanes, **when it's safe to do so.**

But, as we said, that's just for 1% of junctions. The odd ones out. The one-way streets and the *keep right* arrows. For the rest, for the 99%, remember it's: **keep left unless you're turning right or overtaking.**

So, if there aren't any arrows telling you which lane to use, go by the General Rule and assume that the left-hand lane's for turning left and going straight-ahead, and that the right-hand lane's for overtaking and turning right.

Now, turning right is always trickier than turning left. So, when you're turning right:

- If there's a dedicated lane for turning right, use it
- If there's a choice of lanes, generally use the right-hand one
- If you're exiting a one-way street, keep over to the right-hand kerb
- In two-way traffic, if there isn't a choice of lanes but there is a centre white line, move across so that you're positioned just to the left of it
- But if there isn't a centre line then just keep over to the left…

…Because a common mistake, wherever there isn't a centre line, is for guys turning right to be too far over to the right. So don't guess where the middle of the road is. Don't guess where the centre line should be. Just stay over to the left.

So that's turning right and overtaking on the right.

What about overtaking on the left? Overtaking on the left is called *undertaking* and isn't generally allowed. However, you are **allowed to undertake** if you're:

- In a one-way street
- The vehicle ahead of you is turning right
- In a traffic jam and the left-hand lane is moving more freely than the right-hand lane

*

However, the simplest form of overtaking is passing parked cars, which leads us on to something else that your Examiner will be watching for on test, something known as...

Clearance From Stationary Vehicles

Clearance means finding the right balance between the distance you are from any potential danger and the speed you're doing.

If you're able to stay a couple of metres away from, say, a row of parked cars, then you can usually drive at-or-around the speed limit. But if you're forced in closer – and especially if it's to within door-opening range – then you need to slow right down – and we're talking *right* down.

Car doors are massive. If you're looking at the front of a car as its doors open, it's like watching Dumbo's ears unfurl on the big screen. Huge things. So give them plenty of room. Cars not ears. In fact, when you're out-n-about, make a point of watching to see just how big car doors really are. Then, every time you pass a parked car, imagine what it'd look like with a door open, and drive accordingly.

Generally, when dealing with parked cars, try to move out to pass them nice-n-early, so that you're parallel with them as you pass by. But if, instead, you wait until you're close to a parked car before lurching out around it, then the front of your car will swing out into the road, meaning you'll take up far more road-space, making your car seem far wider than it really is.

Clearance, remember, is the balance between your distance from danger and the speed you're doing. Your Examiner doesn't mind you driving through narrow gaps, provided you ease through them nice-n-slowly.

And when passing parked cars either slow down or else give them plenty of room.

Another traffic priority situation is…

Meeting Other Traffic

When a vehicle is parked on your side of the road you have to give-way to any oncoming traffic before pulling out onto the wrong side of the road to overtake that parked vehicle.

And, in that situation, if you have to stop and wait for the oncoming traffic to pass, as we discussed in Lesson 8, wait with your right indicator on, a couple of car lengths back from the parked car, and out towards the centre of the road. This gives you the best possible view along the road, and also lets other traffic know what you're waiting to do.

It follows, then, that if the parked cars are on the other side of the road, then **you have priority** over oncoming traffic. They should wait for you. Should. Sometimes, however, folk don't wait…

Priority is something *given* to you by other drivers, and some of them are not that generous! Maybe they're just being a bully. In that case, grit your teeth and let it go. No *colourful* hand gestures, please!

But sometimes, the driver coming towards you may have already *committed* themselves to passing, say, a row of parked cars, long before they've seen you coming. In that case, try to remember that *sometimes you wait for other traffic and sometimes other traffic waits for you.* It balances itself out. So wait. And if the approaching driver waves their *thanks* to you, wave back.

Okay, but what about when there are parked cars on both sides of the road?

Well, then neither side has priority, so it generally comes down to **first-come, first-served**. In other words, whoever gets there first expects to go through the gap first.

But it doesn't always work like that...

Sometimes, when you're clearly going to reach the gap first – well ahead of the other driver – it becomes painfully obvious that they have no intention of waiting for you. Instead, they just move on out and aim straight for you!

Remember, priority is *given* to you. So, in a situation where priority should be given to you but isn't, don't let it annoy you, instead try to think *defensively*. Protect yourself, both from a potential crash or an argument. I mean, is it really worth the hassle over a few seconds?

Also, on test, if you find yourself face-to-face with some bully flying through a gap towards you – and it becomes a problem – there's only one person your Examiner can fail, and that's you. So, yes...I know it can be annoying...but, as I said – think defensively – and just let it go.

Another situation that can get tricky, is dealing with...

Pedestrians At Junctions

Think of our T-junction again. Picture the major road's footpath and the way it's been split by the minor road. And remember the white lines there: first the hazard line, then both the give-way line and the carriageway line, and the way they're painted *across* the face of the minor road.

Now, imagine replacing those two lines – the give-way line and the carriageway line – with a **zebra crossing**, a crossing linking the two side of the major road's footpath together.

Take a moment to picture it: a zebra crossing, following the course of the major road...

Then picture it across every single junction in the country.

Now, what you're picturing is the way every junction should work...

The major road has priority through the junction, and so does the major road's footpath – just as if there was a zebra crossing there.

So, drivers turning off, or emerging onto, the major road should give-way to pedestrians either crossing – **or clearly waiting to cross** – the minor road, using our virtual zebra crossing.

But there's that word again: *should*. Drivers *should* give way to pedestrians. But we all know – *don't we?* – that many car drivers completely ignore that rule. I mean, how many times have you been out walking and had to dash across the road at a junction because a driver clearly had no intention of waiting for you to cross, even though you had priority?

But, to be fair, sometimes it can be tricky for us drivers...

If a pedestrian's standing there, at the junction, but they don't start to cross, then you have a decision to make. Should you stop and wait for that pedestrian, or do you think it'd be better to *clear* the junction? Maybe the pedestrian's standing at the kerb, yet they're looking down at their phone, not the traffic. Or perhaps there's another car, bearing down on you from behind, and you feel it'd be too dangerous for you to stop for the pedestrian.

And remember that *The Highway Code* tells us **not** to wave pedestrians across the road. So, if a pedestrian's looking at you, hoping you're going to let them cross, but they're hesitating, waiting for a signal from you – a wave of the hand – well, you're not supposed to give that signal. All you can do is slow down and stop, if necessary, but you have to leave the final decision to cross up to the pedestrian themselves. And anyway, the last thing you want is one of those situations where you're waving at each other, both wanting the other to go first!

So, take your time around pedestrians, and use your judgement as to whether you should give-way or move on. The important thing is that, at the end of the test, if your Examiner says that you made a mistake, you should feel able to stand by your decision and say that, in the circumstances, you thought you did the right thing.

Finally, then, for this lesson, we'll round things up by talking about…

Basic Left And Right Turns

Let's start with emerging from the minor road and turning left.

Try to approach the give-way junction keeping neatly over to the left, unless there are parked cars in your way, in which case pass them safely then move over to the left.

A couple of car lengths away from the junction, start taking account of what you can see – so how far you can see into the junction and how busy it is.

If your view's good, and it looks clear of traffic, shift into 2nd gear, take another careful look both ways – and if it's still clear – just carry on.

But if you can see that you're going to have to give-way, or your view of the junction's blocked by parked cars or a hedge, then press the clutch down, let the speed drop right down to a walking pace, and go for 1st gear instead. Then, keeping the clutch down, coast up to the junction, all the while looking left and right, making up your mind as to whether or not you'll be able to keep going.

This is the *passive* part of your junction sequence: clutch down, coasting, looking left and right, accessing the junction, accessing the traffic.

And, yes, look **both** ways, even when you're *only* turning left. Remember, traffic coming from your left that's passing parked cars is likely to be on the *wrong* side of the road – but they're on the wrong side of the *major* road so they still have priority.

Oh, and never trust a left indicator from a car coming from your right...

If you emerge, assuming it's definitely turning left, and there's a crash because – as it turns out – the car didn't turn left, then the crash is considered to be your fault for pulling out, not the other driver's for indicating carelessly.

When it's safe to emerge, whether or not you're stationary, now move into the *positive* phase of the sequence: so release the brakes and ease the clutch up enough to get your engine pulling you forward again. The idea is to emerge – to cross the line – being *driven* forward by your engine, not to just coast out into the major road.

Then keep the clutch still while you steer. **Roughly speaking, the clutch comes up fully at about the same time as you straighten the steering.** A lot of new drivers try to lift the clutch fully within the first couple of **metres** of leaving the junction, while experienced drivers allow themselves a couple of **car lengths** before the clutch is up fully.

Now, emerging and turning right is basically the same as turning left, except, if possible, position your car over to the right, which on a two-way street is just to the left of centre.

But, whether you're turning left or right, when you're emerging, if your view of the junction's blocked, you will have to *creep-n-peep*. Creep-n-peep! That sounds a bit dodgy! But don't panic! It just means **creeping** your car forward, controlling the clutch, while leaning your body forward, looking – **peeping** – to see if the road's clear. It's only when you're sure it's clear that you can safely drive away.

Approaching a major road from a minor road, whether turning left or right, is made more difficult if you're driving uphill. This is where the **holding point technique**, discussed in Lesson 6, really comes into its own.

The idea is to press the clutch down and coast up to the junction, losing speed, changing down into 1st gear, all the while allowing momentum to keep you rolling up to the junction.

Try not to panic about rolling back. After all, if your car's moving forwards, it has to stop first before it can roll back! But new drivers tend to worry that they'll just suddenly start falling backwards, down the hill.

As you arrive at the junction, your speed now dropping away to a walking pace, ease the clutch back up to *catch* the car, just before it stops. That way you can either hold still or creep forward, ready to positively drive onto the major road.

But if you're forced to stop for any more than a few seconds, or if you do start to roll back, press the clutch back down and use the footbrake to hold still. Then use the handbrake, until you're finally ready to move away again, and do a normal hill-start.

The final point on emerging is that, once you've pulled out onto the major road, try to **accelerate** *briskly*. It's not good enough to just pull out into an otherwise adequate gap in traffic – so giving everyone plenty of room – but to then hold traffic up by not accelerating.

So, emerging at a give-way junction:

- Approach planning on trying to keep moving
- Look both ways
- Find a suitable gap to emerge safely
- When you emerge, try to accelerate

So that's emerging. Now let's talk about turning in from the major road to the minor road.

Again, when turning left, try to keep close to the kerb on both the approach to, and the exit from, the turn. Try not to either bump the kerb or wander across the hazard line.

And when turning right, try to avoid **cutting the corner**. Cutting the corner means turning in too soon and going onto the wrong side of the road. So, wait until you reach the centre of the road you're turning into – usually shown by its hazard line – before steering in. And if you have to wait for oncoming traffic to pass, wait with the front of your car in line with the minor road's hazard line.

Then, as you turn into the side road, look along its left-hand kerb to help with your steering as you straighten up. Remember, you go where you look, so look where you want to go. But if you look at the hazard line as you turn in, then you're likely to drift onto that line.

Turning into a side road, either left or right, is usually done in 2nd gear. And it's also usually done with the clutch up. Changing down into 2nd, then bringing the clutch back up, will give you loads of engine braking and help you keep your speed and steering under control.

But sometimes, on really tight turns, it might be necessary to use the **controlled coasting technique**, also from Lesson 6.

This involves slowing right down, to below 10mph, but rather than changing down into 1st gear, simply using 2nd but holding the clutch down, coasting around the corner, controlling your speed with the brakes. Then, as you straighten up to drive away from the junction, give the engine a bit of gas and ease the clutch back up.

Now, just before turning into a side road, take a moment to look into it through your side window to see what's going on in the new road, to see what you're letting yourself in for. Maybe there are pedestrians crossing the road, or parked cars to nip round. But, whatever, try to avoid turning into a side road just looking solely through your windscreen. If you do, by the time you catch sight of those pedestrians or parked cars it might be too late to deal with them safely.

As for steering, as you prepare to turn, lift your hand – depending on the way you want to turn – high up on the steering-wheel, so that you can get a good initial pull down on the wheel. The idea is to steer in quickly. When you're halfway round a corner, it's much easier to take steering off than it is to put more on. Also, if you steer in quickly, it means you can be more relaxed about straightening up. You'll have more time. But if you steer in slowly, you'll find yourself playing catch-up with the steering all the way around the corner.

Okay, so a quick recap:

- Remember to use your mirrors
- Remember to carefully time your indicators
- Remember to watch for pedestrians
- Remember that Examiners are in no hurry, so take your time.

Now, this has been a marathon lesson, but let's finish-up by boiling everything we've covered down into four words:

- Mirror
- Signal
- Speed
- Gear

So, the way it works: think about the junction you're approaching and the way you're going to position your car. Then:

- Check your mirrors
- Think about the timing of any signals you intend to give
- Slow down
- Change down.

Mirror, signal, speed, gear.

And finally…

Examiners are slow to fail people who drive too slow, but they're quick to fail people who drive too quick.

Take your time.

MARK JOHNSTON

ROUNDABOUTS

Lesson 10

I hope that if you were able to practise after Lesson 9 that the drives went well, that they weren't too stressful!

Now, in this lesson, we'll be talking about priority, and also the system of lanes and signals, at roundabouts. Then we'll move on to:

- The Approach
- The Zone
- Roundabouts on Test
- Mini roundabouts

Let's get started.

A roundabout, then, is essentially a small one-way system with a flowerbed in the middle! The road going round the flowerbed is the major road. The roads joining the roundabout are minor roads.

So, even if you've been driving along a main road for miles, when you meet a roundabout your road becomes the minor road and you must give-way to traffic already on the roundabout, so coming round from your right.

Approaching a roundabout, lanes and signals work in the same way as they do for any other type of junction...

So, to choose your **lane,** use the General Rule, discussed in Lesson 9: keep left, unless you're turning right or overtaking, or where painted arrows show otherwise.

Signalling is also the same as for other types of junctions…

So, indicate on the approach if you're planning on turning either left or right, but when you're going straight-ahead at a roundabout the *signal* for that is to NOT *indicate!*

There's no flashing amber light in the middle of your bonnet – no indicator for straight-ahead!

But where roundabouts are different from other types of junctions is that on a roundabout you signal twice. Once, as you approach, and then again as you leave the roundabout…

Always exit a roundabout indicating left. It doesn't matter where you've come from or where you're going to – in all but a tiny number of cases – indicate left as you exit…

The left indicator as you leave a roundabout is given as a courtesy to those drivers waiting to join. It lets them know you're leaving and that they can take your place. It's like politely holding a door open for someone.

*

Now, you may have noticed that, like other junctions, roundabouts are not always uniform. They vary. And in your area, and the area in which you'll be taking your test, there's going to be one-or-two roundabouts that aren't necessarily clear-cut, where you're going to have to pull over and discuss how to deal with them with your Supervisor.

But, bearing that in mind, let's run through how roundabouts generally work:

- Turning Left, the 1st exit:
- Approach in the left lane, indicating left
- Keep to the left as you emerge onto the roundabout
- Keep your left indicator on as you leave

- Going straight-ahead, 2nd exit:
- Approach left lane, no indicator
- Keep to the left as you emerge
- Indicate left as you pass the road before the one you're taking
- Leave by the left lane, indicating left

- Turning Right, 3rd exit:
- Approach right lane, indicating right
- Emerge onto the right lane
- Indicate left as you pass the road before the one you're taking
- Change lanes, exiting in the left lane, left indicator

Remember, though, that the General Rule says that at junctions you can use the right-hand lane to overtake, as well as for turning right.

And it's the same on roundabouts...

If a roundabout has two lanes on the approach and two on the exit – provided there aren't any signs or road markings telling you otherwise – it's okay to use the right-hand lane as an overtaking lane. And if you do, signal in the same way as you would for straight-ahead normally – so no indicator on the approach but then a left indicator as you pass the exit before the one you intend to take – then exit the roundabout in the most convenient lane.

Now let's discuss roundabouts in a more practical sense. And let's begin by again talking about...

The Approach

If possible, sort your lane out nice-n-early and, if necessary, use the **breaking the signal** technique. So indicate for any lane change – switch it off for a few seconds – then indicate a second time for the roundabout itself.

Then, engine braking. Come off the gas to let your engine settle the car down. This will make the approach more relaxed and controlled, rather than just flying up and going from gas to brake in a mad panic.

Next, the gears. If you're joining the back of a queue then just shift down into 1st gear as you arrive. But if you think it might be possible to keep going at the roundabout, then change down into 2nd just before you reach the point where the road kicks round to the left, just before the roundabout itself. Then you'll be able to use *controlled coasting* – so, clutch down, controlling the rolling with the brake – for the last couple of car lengths, as you look for your chance to join the roundabout.

But keep an eye on the car in front of you...

No, seriously. It's one of our most common crashes: running into the guy in front at a roundabout. Happens all the time.

And it's such a common crash simply because drivers are looking for a gap in traffic – then driving off when they spot one – before the guy in front's even moved! So, make sure the guy ahead of you is definitely moving-away before you look to your right, before you start looking for your gap.

But then, don't only look to your right...

Because you go where you look. If you spend all your time looking to your right then you'll move to your right, out of your lane. So, take your time and split where you're looking between your windscreen – to keep your steering accurate – and your side window, to check...

The Zone

The *Zone*, here, is the bit of the roundabout to your immediate right. So, if you imagine a roundabout as a clock face – and you're approaching from six o'clock – then the zone is the bit that goes round anticlockwise to your three o'clock.

That's the area we're interested in.

That's your zone.

And the guys in your zone have priority.

So how do you get onto the roundabout – it all looks so busy – when's it your turn?

There are three main possibilities for joining a roundabout...

- A clear zone
- A car in the zone but it's indicating left
- A car on the *far side*

Okay. Let's run through those three.

First: a clear zone. Fairly self-explanatory, I suppose, but note that a clear zone doesn't necessarily mean there's no traffic at all to your right. There could be vehicles waiting to join the roundabout from the road over to your right. But they're still *waiting* to join the roundabout. They're not actually on it yet. Remember, your zone refers to the roundabout itself; it doesn't include the road leading up to the roundabout.

Second: there's a car in the zone but it's indicating left. So you have a driver who's very kindly letting you know that he's leaving the roundabout before he reaches you, letting you know that you can take his place.

Finally, third: *the far side.* The idea is that traffic joining the roundabout from directly opposite you, and going straight-ahead to exit the roundabout onto the road you're coming from, will be in *their* left-hand lane for the entire roundabout – so over on the far side as you look at them – and **unlikely** to swing round towards you.

But, unfortunately, all of these options generally involve you driving into a gap, rather than the entire roundabout being completely clear...

Picture one of those luggage carousels at an airport, the things you pick your cases up from after a flight. Now imagine it was your job to load all the bags from the plane onto the conveyor belt. You've had a tough day, you're tired, but this is the last flight you have to unload, and you've now got just one more suitcase to put on the conveyor before you finish work. But the conveyor's full. Still, never mind, here comes the passengers, and the conveyor starts to move...

So, there you are, waiting with that last suitcase. Now, are you just watching all those bags as they trundle past you, or are you looking for a gap?

Well, a roundabout's like that. Try not to just stare at the traffic. Instead, look for a gap to move into. So look behind the car to your right – for a gap – not directly at it. At busy times of the day, getting onto a roundabout can be tricky. If you want it to be completely clear then you could be in for a long wait.

To recap: don't worry too much about the traffic waiting to join the roundabout from the road over to your right. Those guys are the same as you – they're still on the minor road – so they don't have priority over you until they move onto the roundabout and into your zone.

And don't worry about that guy in your zone, the one who's indicating left. They're telling you that they're leaving your zone before they reach you.

And don't worry too much about that car over on the far side of the roundabout. Chances are, it's going straight-ahead, leaving by the road you're joining from.

And don't worry about that one lonely car on an otherwise

deserted roundabout, the one now in your zone, because, with careful timing, you can join the roundabout immediately behind it, without having to stop.

But one final word about your zone. Note that we're NOT talking about lanes here, because the zone is all the lanes to your right.

So, if you're turning left, don't fall into the trap of only looking at the lane nearest to you, thinking of it as *your* lane. Because it isn't. A driver, to your right, using the lane nearest the roundabout, can change lanes and move across towards you at any moment. They're already on the roundabout. It's *their* lane – if they want it – not yours.

Now let's talk about the way your Examiner will direct you at…

Roundabouts On Your Test

They might say, *at the roundabout, I'd like you to turn left. That's the first exit, sign-posted London.*

Or, *at the roundabout, I'd like you to go straight-ahead. That's the second exit, sign-posted Glasgow.*

So you're given nice clear directions. But if you still find yourself feeling unsure about where you're going, it's okay for you to ask your Examiner to repeat the direction, or even to ask for further clarification if you want more detail. It's super important that you're clear in your own mind exactly where you're going, before you enter the roundabout.

But, on the other hand, you're not being tested on your ability to follow directions…

So, if you do make a mistake, and you realise you're in the wrong lane, just go wherever the lane you're now in leads you. Provided you use the lanes and your indicators correctly – for the exit that you're now taking – you won't be marked down, even if you're now merrily heading off in the wrong direction!

However, you will be marked down if, on realising your mistake, you attempt some kind of crazy last-minute lane change. That would be dangerous driving. That would be a test fail.

*

Now, mirrors, as you know, are a really big deal on test. So it's obviously important to use the mirrors correctly on roundabouts...

Firstly, use the mirror, signal, manoeuvre routine as you approach a roundabout.

Then, if you're going straight-ahead, on the roundabout itself, use the rear-view mirror before indicating left, then the left door-mirror as you finally leave the roundabout.

When you're turning right, and you reach the point where you need to start your lane change – to move from the right-hand lane over to the left – you've got a whole lot to do:

- Check your rear-view mirror
- Switch your indicators from right to left
- Use your left-hand door mirror
- Glance to your left-hand blind-spot

...and all in those few seconds!

Finally a quick word about...

Mini Roundabouts

These are the small ones – funnily enough – that are simply a painted circle on the road. They have an additional sign that you'll see on the approach: a **blue circle showing three arrows arranged around it**. This sign's telling you that you must drive clockwise around the painted circle, not over it or to the right of it.

Another road-sign you'll often see when approaching a mini-roundabout is a written one that says, **_give way to the right_**.

As you know, on a full-sized roundabout you give way to traffic **_in your zone_**. But on a mini-roundabout you also need to be wary of traffic approaching the roundabout, because often those guys will approach really quickly, flying onto the mini roundabout. So, be really careful, and take a moment to look a bit further down the road, rather than just focusing on your zone.

Signalling also differs on a mini-roundabout compared to a full-sized one because you only need to indicate for a mini-roundabout on the approach to it. They're so tight there isn't time to indicate left as you're leaving it, even after a right turn.

Okay, so that's roundabouts. Like everything else in this driving lark, take your time. It sounds like a contradiction, but if you approach roundabouts slowly you'll actually get around them quicker because you won't need to stop so often.

So, approach carefully, watch out for the traffic in front of you, and try to work out what's happening in your zone.

Now it's onto Lesson 11, and traffic lights.

MARK JOHNSTON

TRAFFIC LIGHTS

Lesson 11

In this lesson we're first going to be discussing priority at traffic lights then we'll move onto...

- Sequence
- Filter arrows and filter lanes
- Slip lanes
- Pedestrian crossings
- Sensors
- Turning right
- Turning left

The purpose of traffic lights is to alternate priority at busy junctions. So the folk with the green light have priority, the ones on red wait. Then the lights change and it swaps around. Then the lights change again and the pedestrians get their turn, and so on.

When you're approaching traffic lights use the General Rule we first discussed in lesson 9. So, keep to the left unless you're turning right or overtaking, except where road arrows show otherwise. And, on test, note that your Examiner will only direct you at traffic lights when they want you to turn either left or right. They won't tell you to go straight-ahead. They'll expect you to do that for yourself. So, when you're out practising, remind your Supervisor to keep quiet at lights, unless they want you to turn.

As you approach a green light, be prepared for them to change.

Traffic lights don't change *suddenly*, they just *change*. It's what they do. So be ready. But, approaching green, being *ready* doesn't necessarily mean slowing down. Being ready is often just a mental preparation thing.

In thirty limits, it's usually okay to stay at a constant speed, but to keep one eye on the lights. Slowing down when the lights are still at green will just irritate following traffic, causing them to get even closer to your back bumper than they already are.

Now let's talk about...

Sequence

It goes...

- Green
- Amber
- Red
- Red and Amber
- Green

Green means go. Everybody knows that. Ah...but it means *go* provided there's somewhere for you to *actually* go to. It doesn't just mean pull forward into a queue and block the junction. So, if there's a traffic jam ahead of you, wait behind the white line until there's enough room to cross the junction fully.

Next is amber. Amber on its own. **Amber means stop**.

So amber DOESN'T mean *prepare to stop*.

But then it doesn't mean panic, and launch into some wild emergency stop, either.

Amber means stop, ***provided you can stop safely before you reach the white line***. But if you genuinely feel as though you can't stop safely, it's okay to keep going. That's what amber's for.

Sometimes, when folk get stopped by a nice policeman, one who tells them that he saw them *jump the lights*, they reply that they were *only* amber. This tells the nice policeman that they don't actually know what the amber light means! Maybe if instead they were to say, *I saw the lights change to amber but I didn't think I could stop safely in time*, our nice policeman might be a little more forgiving!

Amber is on for just a couple of seconds and is followed by red.

Red means stop.

Red means stop before the line. It's illegal – so you'd fail your test – to cross the line on red. Notice that the white line is a solid line, a **stop line**, not just a give-way line. When you're waiting at red, keep still – none of that creeping forward lark.

And wait with your handbrake on and the gears in neutral. And if you're in a queue, wait where you can see the tyres of the car ahead of you. Don't get too close. You're aiming to make your Examiner feel as comfortable as possible.

Red and amber together means get ready to go. Again, it's on for just a couple of seconds. Bit of a waste of time, this one! In fact, in some countries they don't bother with it at all, they just go directly from red to green. And that kind of makes sense... I mean, if red and amber together means *get ready to go* it's no wonder some drivers mistakenly think amber on its own means *get ready to stop!*

Anyway...green, amber, red, red and amber together, green. That's your sequence. So if you see amber on its own then next is going to be red.

Now, at some lights, as well as the three main lights we've just discussed, you'll see another light alongside green, making an 'L' shape. These are...

Filter Arrows And Filter Lanes

Filter arrows are additional green lights, a little bonus green light. They are not to be confused with those junctions that have multiple separate traffic lights.

Filter arrows to the **right** come on either with or after the main green. They're there to tell you that the oncoming traffic now has a red light – so they should stop – allowing you to turn right. Right filter arrows don't always have their own lane, sometimes you share with traffic going straight-ahead.

But where there's a **left** filter arrow, there will also be a left filter *lane* – a separate lane with a painted turn left arrow.

Left filter arrows usually come on while the main light is still at red, allowing just the traffic turning left to go. The green filter arrow then stays on until the main lights change to green. At that point, the filter arrow is no longer needed because – when the main light's at green – **all traffic** facing that light can go, so the filter arrow goes out.

A mistake learners often make is to see the left filter arrow come on, but to then continue watching just that one light – the green arrow – as they approach the junction. So then, if the arrow goes out, they stop, because they've been so focused on that filter arrow that they haven't noticed that the main green has come on...

It's the red light coming on that tells you to stop, not the green arrow going out.

Filter arrows to the right come on either with or after the main green. They're there to tell you that the oncoming traffic now has a red light – so they should stop – allowing you to turn right. Right filter arrows don't always have their own lane, sometimes you share with traffic going straight-ahead.

And sometimes there's a completely separate lane that heads off to the left just before you reach the white stop line. These are...

Slip Lanes

...and they take you away from the main traffic light junction to bring you to their own junction instead. Usually slip lanes end in a give-way line, but sometimes they have their own, separate, traffic light. And sometimes they have a traffic-light-controlled pedestrian-crossing halfway down them, followed by a give-way line.

When slip lanes end in a give-way line, you must give-way to traffic coming from the main junction, which is now to your right.

Slip lanes help keep things flowing by allowing traffic to turn left even when the main junction light is at red. Which is a good thing. But a bad thing is that sometimes pedestrians casually cross the slip lane, mistakenly assuming that when the **green man on the main junction** is on, that it also protects them on the slip lane. But it doesn't. Not necessarily. The slip lane is separate from the main junction.

All of which brings us neatly onto...

Pedestrians

If you take a look at the white stop line at a traffic light junction, you'll see that just after it there are usually two rows of metal studs set into the road surface. They mark the pedestrian crossing area. Most lights have a pedestrian crossing across each of its roads, so a crossroads usually has four crossings.

The idea is that, when someone presses the *pedestrian* button at the junction, intending to summon the *green man*, the computer controlling the lights will, at some point during its cycle, stop all the traffic with red lights then light-up the green man. And the pedestrians cross.

So is the green man just for pedestrians and has nothing to do with drivers? No…

Okay, so when the green man's on, all the traffic should be stationary at red. But what about if a driver's in the middle of the junction, waiting to turn right, when their light turns red and the green man comes on?

Well, then it would be up to that driver to have noticed that the green man has come on and to give-way to any pedestrians who are crossing or waiting to cross. So, yes, drivers do need to keep an eye on the green man, as well as the main traffic lights.

Now, as we've discussed, the pedestrian's green man only comes on if someone has pressed the button. The button sends a signal to the computer controlling the lights, letting it know that somebody wants to cross…

Well, as you approach the traffic lights in your car, you press a *kind of* button, too. Or, at least, your car does. Because, as you motor up to the lights, you're driving across a series of…

Sensors

…which are laid into the road surface, sending signals to that computer, letting it know that you're arriving at the junction. You'll see them as lines of shiny tarmac, starting ten-to-fifteen metres back from the stop line. They can look as if they're just scars, leftover from long-finished road-works. Every road, approaching every traffic light junction has them, at least three sets of them, constantly updating the computer about the flow of traffic.

So, traffic lights don't just change randomly. You'll see this most clearly if you approach a red light at four o'clock in the morning. Then, provided you're not speeding, as you arrive at the lights they'll be changing to green, good as gold.

Four in the afternoon, however, is a different story. The dreaded school run is in full swing and the poor computer's struggling to keep things moving. So, eventually it becomes overwhelmed and goes into a default mode of, say, sixty seconds for this road then sixty seconds for the other road.

Right filter arrows, as we've already said, often come on simultaneously with the main green.

But, at other junctions, right filter arrows come on after the main green has been on for a while. At these junctions, there's an additional sensor immediately after both the white line and the pedestrian crossing. It's usually the size and shape of a living-room rug, and its job is to tell the computer that the right-turn traffic is building up. So, essentially, it switches the right filter arrow on.

So, when you're sitting first in the queue, waiting at red, waiting to turn right – and you can see that the lights have that distinctive 'L' shape – look at the road surface ahead of you to see if there's an additional sensor there. Then, if there is, when the lights change to green and you move forward, if the filter arrow hasn't come on, wait right there, right on top of that sensor, to let the computer know you're waiting for the arrow to help you finish the turn.

But, what about if you're…

Turning Right

…and there isn't a green filter arrow?

We started this lesson talking about priority, and the way traffic lights alternate priority. So at lights, the road on green is the major road.

But remember there are *two* priority rules at junctions. In Lesson 9, we covered the two questions you should ask yourself about priority as you approach a bog-standard junction…

The first, related to the major road.

But the second question was: *who's turning right?* And this second rule also comes into play here, at traffic lights.

A green light gives you permission to enter the junction.

But if you're turning right, you must still give-way to oncoming traffic.

When you get the green light, pull forward to the other side of the pedestrian crossing area and, if there's oncoming traffic, wait there.

You're waiting for one of three things…

- A gap in the oncoming traffic
- Your light going back to red and the oncoming traffic stopping
- Or, if there is one, a right filter arrow

Note that if there is a right filter arrow then you don't need to wait for it to come on in order to finish your turn – a gap in oncoming traffic will do – the filter arrow is just there to help you if you get stuck on the junction.

And, of course, the fourth thing to watch out for, as we discussed a moment ago, is for any pedestrians who are crossing the junction ahead of you as you make your turn.

Once you've crossed the white line and positioned yourself for the right turn, you're committed now to completing the turn. So, even if your light turns red, you're expected to finish your turn, to clear the junction, to get out of the way, ideally before the next line of traffic starts moving.

So, yes, you need your wits about you. From your light changing to red, to the next line of traffic moving away again on their green, it's only five-or-six seconds. That's all the time you get.

Now, in Lesson 9, we discussed turning right at crossroads and the choice of turning either **left-to-left** or **right-to-right**...

When turning right, left-to-left is turning across the front of the traffic opposite you that's also turning right, and right-to-right involves passing those guys in a straight line then moving round to the right once you're behind them.

And, in Lesson 9, we also said that left-to-left is by far the most common way right turns at junctions are done, and especially at traffic lights...

So, picture the scene: you're waiting at red, waiting to turn right, and there's traffic opposite you, also waiting to turn right. The lights change. So you move forward across your white line and onto the pedestrian crossing area. The plan then is to angle round to the right, moving forward just enough to look past the driver opposite, the one who's also turning right...

And that driver will hopefully do the same. If you had a *birds-eye* view of the junction, the idea is that you and the driver opposite each take-up a third of the junction, but that you leave the middle third clear, so that you can see past one-another and, when it's safe, have space to drive away.

Ah, but what about if the traffic opposite isn't turning right? Maybe there isn't even a road there for them to turn right into! Then, in that case, on your green, come forward **perfectly straight**, no movement to the right whatsoever, making sure you don't get in their way.

Turning right at traffic lights, then, is tricky. There's lots going on. The good news, though, is that...

Turning Left

…is easier.

The main thing is to watch out for cyclists. They'll sneak up between you and the kerb and might not notice your indicator. Ah…indicators. I mean, why do so many drivers wait until the lights change to green, and they're moving again, before they think to indicate? The indicators are there to tell people what you're going to do next, not what you're doing now. Sticking an indicator on a split-second before turning left is no use to anyone. And remember, that includes when you're in a lane which only goes in that one direction.

Anyway, let's end this lesson by telling you something that you already know: that jumping lights is pretty much the most dangerous habit you can get into. So, don't be an *amber gambler*, as the TV advert-thing used to say, back-in-the-day.

But some drivers do choose to take that risk. And not *just* risk jumping amber lights, either. They might start with amber lights, but it isn't long before they graduate on to: *they've only just changed to red, so I've still got ages yet.*

Unfortunately, nowadays, it's not unusual to see *your* light change to green while cross traffic is still merrily going over the junction.

But, the thing is, those folk jumping the lights always assume that you will be stationary, that you will wait for them, and that you will then move away nice-n-slowly, once *they've* finished.

But what if you're not stationary? What if you're approaching the junction in the overtaking lane, doing 40mph, when the lights change? You thinking, *that was good timing,* as the guy coming from your left jumps a light that's already been red for five seconds…

It always goes wrong eventually.

And on that cheerful note...

MARK JOHNSTON

DUAL CARRIAGEWAYS AND MOTORWAYS

Lesson 12

In this lesson we'll discuss:

- Lane discipline
- Undertaking
- Following distances
- Slip lanes
- Junctions

But first: what is a ***dual carriageway***? Well, it's a road that isn't a motorway but looks a bit like one!

- ***Dual*** here means two
- ***Carriageway*** means a strip of tarmac

So, a *dual carriageway* has two strips of tarmac, running parallel with each other, with a barrier between them.

This barrier, also like a motorway, is often a strip of grass lined with an Armco *crash* barrier, and is known as a ***central reservation***. And dual carriageways also, again, same as motorways, often have an emergency lane, known as a ***hard shoulder***.

Dual carriageways, again, same as motorways, are described by counting the lanes in each carriageway. So, if each carriageway on a dual carriageway is divided into two lanes by a lane-line then it's known as a two-lane dual-carriageway.

And, finally, both dual carriageways and motorways have a national speed limit for cars and motorbikes of 70mph.

So motorways and dual carriageways have many similarities. However, for us, as learner drivers, the main difference is that:

- You can drive on a dual carriageway with your Supervisor or Instructor, and you might be taken onto a dual carriageway on your test
- But you can only drive on a motorway with an Approved Driving Instructor (ADI) until after you've passed your test

Route signs on dual carriageways are the same as on other main roads: so green backgrounds to show the towns and cities that are further along the road, and white background signs for local destinations.

Motorways use blue signs.

So, countdown markers, for example, on dual carriageways have white diagonal stripes on a green background. Motorways have white on blue. For both, though, each diagonal stripe represents 100 yards to, say, a slip lane, for example.

But, when it comes to junctions, the main difference between motorways and dual carriageways is that, although both of them do use slip lanes, dual carriageways also use *normal* give-way style junctions, including right turns and roundabouts...

Motorways don't. Motorways occasionally *merge* – when two of them come together – but they generally use slip lanes, positioned over to the far left-hand side of the road, to both leave and join them.

The left-hand lane on motorways and dual carriageways is often known as the *slow* lane, and the lane over to the right, the one closest to the central reservation, is known as the *fast* lane. And then, if there are three lanes, the middle one's called the…middle lane! Ah, but all the lanes have the same speed limit, so there isn't really either a slow lane or a fast lane. The left-hand lane's for anybody to use, while the lanes to the right of it are for overtaking.

So the lanes are more accurately described by numbering them. The left lane, then, the *slow* lane, is Lane 1. The lanes to the right of Lane 1 are then numbered accordingly…Lane 2, Lane 3…

So, note that on motorways Lane 2 is for overtaking Lane 1. But on dual carriageways, Lane 2 can also be for **turning right.** Something to consider when you're bombing down a dual carriageway in Lane 2, closing in on the slowcoach up ahead, thinking you're in the *fast* lane. That *slowcoach* might be about to brake and make a right turn!

As we've already said, as a learner driver, you're not yet allowed on motorways unless you're with an ADI, but you are allowed on dual carriageways, and you'll probably drive on one on your test.

So, on test, if you find yourself catching up with a slower moving vehicle, and, again, conditions allow, you're expected to overtake. That means moving over one lane to your right.

Try to move over nice-n-early. Try to keep up a nice steady speed for the lane change. But don't wait until you're virtually on top of the slower vehicle before moving out, because then you'll often be forced to slow down by cars that are overtaking *you*.

So, to move into the overtaking lane, use your mirrors carefully, especially your right door mirror. Then, when you're ready to make your move, indicate. Try to allow your indicators to flash at least three times before you change lanes. Then **glance,** super-quick, to the blind spot directly alongside you, for a final check.

Try to avoid treating lane changes as something you need to slow down for. Try not to lift off the accelerator and let your speed fade away. Okay, yes, sometimes it is necessary to slow down to merge with passing traffic, but generally speaking, lane changing is something best done at a constant speed.

As you overtake, focus on staying in the centre of your lane until you can see the front of the vehicle you've overtaken in your mirrors. Then indicate left, and, if all's good, move back into your original lane.

And moving back to the left, back to Lane 1, so getting out of the way of overtaking traffic, is known as having good…

Lane Discipline

But, generally speaking, our lane disciple, here in the UK, is terrible! Unlike our European neighbours, we have this *fast lane* mentality. They overtake then move immediately back into Lane 1. We don't. We like to hog the fast lane!

Anyway, on test, use the General Rule, so keep to the left, keep to Lane 1, unless you're turning right or overtaking, except where road arrows tell you to do otherwise.

So, drive in Lane 1, move into Lane 2 to overtake, but then, after overtaking, move back into Lane 1. So, we overtake on the right, because overtaking on the left is known as…

Undertaking

…and undertaking's not allowed, unless:

- The driver ahead of you is turning right
- You're in slow traffic, and Lane 1 is moving more freely than Lane 2

The other time you're allowed to pass on the left is on a one-way street, so not something to really concern us here.

But what does concern you, what your Examiner will be

watching for on test, is that you're using the correct lanes while driving along normally and also while overtaking, and also that you demonstrate an awareness of the rules of both lane discipline and undertaking.

Something else your Examiner's going to be watching closely are your…

Following Distances

Have you ever heard the phrase, *only a fool breaks the two-second rule*? No? But I bet your Supervisor has. It used to be on the TV, in the ad breaks, all the time back-in-the-day.

The idea is that as the vehicle you're following passes some easily identifiable landmark – a slip lane or a side road – you literally say to yourself, nice-n-slowly, *one thousand and one, one thousand and two*… and see if you're then passing that same spot in the road. If you are, you're roughly two seconds back from the guy you're following. You're obeying the *two-second rule*.

That two second gap is considered to be the minimum safe following distance for speeds over 40mph on dry roads. On test, if you get any closer, your Examiner will ask you to drop back. And you don't want to hear that – *oh no* – hearing that would almost certainly mean a test fail.

In the wet, you're supposed to double the gap and leave four seconds between you and the guy you're following. And in ice and snow, theory test questions suggest leaving a gap ten times greater than normal. Although, how you're supposed to put that into practise is anyone's guess!

Anyway, as you're likely to drive on a dual carriageway on test, let's look at the different ways of joining and leaving them, and let's start with…

Slip Lanes

…and the main thing to remember, which is that, as much as possible, try to adjust your speed on the actual slip lane, not on the dual carriageway itself. The slip lanes are acceleration and deceleration lanes, so it's in **them** that you should try to adjust your speed.

So, joining a carriageway, try to speed up along the slip lane before joining the main road, lessening the speed differential between you and the traffic already on the carriageway by as much as possible.

If you drive too slowly down an acceleration lane then it can be really tricky joining the faster road. The difference in speeds between you and the other traffic can be really intimidating, making it difficult to judge when there's a suitable gap for you to move into.

So use the *acceleration lane* as the name suggests, and accelerate! Then use your door mirror and indicate right. And, because you'll often be at an acute angle to the carriageway, check your blind-spot two-or-three times, as well, to give you the best possible view of the traffic you're planning on merging with.

But, unfortunately, if you reach the end of the slip lane, so if you reach the carriageway line, and you haven't yet been able to join the main carriageway, then you have a problem because the traffic already on the carriageway has priority so you must give-way.

Now, generally, at a give-way line, in that situation, you'd have to stop and wait, but because here that puts you in a dangerous position, if there is a hard shoulder it's usually best to continue on down it – steady speed, right indicator on – watching your door mirror for a gap.

When you're leaving a carriageway via a slip lane, try to keep your speed up as much as possible on the main road itself. The idea is to do the bulk of your braking, and any gear changing, in the *deceleration* slip-lane after you've left the dual carriageway, to get yourself clear of the guys zooming up behind you.

It's really dangerous to slow down unexpectedly and unnecessarily when traffic behind you could easily be doing 70mph. And it's doubly dangerous when you're turning right, because you'll be using what – as we've already said – some drivers consider to be the *fast* lane.

So, indicate nice-n-early when you're leaving a carriageway, at least a good few seconds before you begin slowing down. And when you're turning right, remember to *break the signal*, a technique we covered in Lesson 8. So, indicate once for the lane change – switch the indicator off – then indicate again for the slip lane or junction itself.

When turning from the carriageway into a side road, try to indicate nice-n-early, ideally before braking. Then slow down for the junction steadily, using your footbrake smoothly, remembering that your brake lights will warn following traffic of what you're planning on doing at the junction.

Slip lanes, then, are used on both motorways and dual-carriageways. But on dual carriageways there are also other types of…

Junctions

There can be roundabouts – which are treated in the same way as roundabouts on other types of roads – and also fairly standard minor-road give-way junctions which don't have a slip lane.

Now, when you're emerging onto the carriageway, and turning left, there are two things to remember:

- Your Examiner generally wants both lanes of traffic coming from your right to be clear, not just the lane nearest to you – in case a car in Lane 2 moves into Lane 1 without indicating
- And, also, you need a sufficient gap in traffic before emerging, to allow yourself chance to get up to a reasonable speed before any traffic already on the carriageway catches up with you

But it's turning right, coming from a minor road, cutting across the dual carriageway, that's the trickiest manoeuvre of them all. Believe me, your Examiner could tell you horror stories about learners tackling these junctions!

Okay, so picture approaching a dual carriageway from a minor road. Now, if there isn't a central reservation wide enough for you to wait in, then you'll need all of the lanes, from both directions, to be clear before you turn right, because you'll have to do the entire thing in one go.

But, if the central reservation's wide enough, then you'll usually be able to cross the two carriageways individually, with a pause in the centre. So, it's a bit easier than taking all four lanes in one go, but it's still tricky…

Okay, so let's call the first carriageway that you're going to cross, the one nearest to you, *Carriageway A*, and the one over on the far side, with traffic coming from your left, *Carriageway B*.

Now, before crossing Carriageway A, you'll need both lanes from your right to be clear. Then, look to your left, along Carriageway B, because – before you cross Carriageway A – **you must also be clear of any traffic coming from Carriageway B that's turning right**. This is super important. Often, even fully-qualified drivers doing this seem to think the idea is to just give way to the right – so Carriageway A – then move into the middle, and *then* give way to the left – Carriageway B. But it isn't…

You must look both ways before crossing Carriageway A.

But remember, you're only giving way to the traffic on Carriageway B **that's turning right**. At this point, you don't need to worry about guys on Carriageway B who are continuing straight through the junction.

Okay. So picture it: you're completely clear from your right, and also clear of any traffic coming from your left that's turning right. Now you can cross Carriageway A...

As you move forward, into the central reservation area, stay fairly straight but with a slight steer over to the right. The aim is to get well into the central reservation, close to the line protecting you from Carriageway B, and then give-way to traffic coming from your left.

Now, if you're roughly at right-angles to Carriageway B, three things generally happen:

- Traffic turning right from Carriageway B can still turn-right by passing you on your left
- You have an easy view of traffic on Carriageway B through your passenger window
- You're not inviting any drivers, who've perhaps followed you across Carriageway A, to pull-up on your left and block your view – they're far more likely to go over to your driver's side

Now you want both lanes from your left to be clear, because the plan is to move over to Lane 1 – the left lane, the slow lane, or whatever you like to call it – to finish the turn.

The plan is **not** to go into Lane 2 unless, that is, the traffic on Carriageway B is at a standstill. In that case, if someone let's you in, it's okay to go into Lane 2, but then you want to move into Lane 1 as soon as possible.

So, crossing a dual carriageway: your Examiner's more

frightened than you are!

COUNTRY ROADS (TAKE ME HOME)

Lesson 13

If your local driving test centre's anywhere near nice green countryside then, chances are, your Examiner's going to take you for a nice little drive through some of it, for ten minutes-or-so. Happy days.

Now, in this lesson, we're essentially going to be talking about three things:

- Speed Limits
- Road positioning
- Overtaking

And, as the list suggests, we'll start with…

Speed Limits

Picture a map of Britain. England, Scotland and Wales. Colour your imaginary map green, to represent all our beautiful green countryside. Now, add to your map grey dots, a dot for each village, town and city in the land, a dot for every place with a name.

Essentially, the way it works is this: 99% of roads across the UK fall into one of two speed-limit groups. The green bits on your imaginary map are called *national speed limit* areas and the grey dots are the residential 30mph limits.

The other 1% of roads have either forty or fifty limits, or one of the 20mph zones that you'll see in some towns and cities. And this 1% is well signposted. Twenty limit zones are marked as you enter the areas, and 40-and-50mph limits also start with a full-sized speed limit sign, which are then backed-up by smaller speed limit signs to act as reminders, called *repeaters*, every few hundred metres-or-so.

The thirty limits, then, are like cosy blankets spread across every village, town and city in the land. So, if you can put a name to where you are – London, Edinburgh, Cardiff – right down to our smallest, most picture-perfect villages, then chances are, the speed limit is thirty. And, as you enter a town, and pass the thirty sign, then that's it – that sign's all you get – there usually aren't any *repeaters*.

But then, if you turn around and leave that same town, on the back of that thirty sign – like the two sides to a coin – you'll see a national speed limit sign. That's the white circle with the black diagonal line across it. And you'll notice that it doesn't have a number on it. That's because the actual speed limit, on a national speed limit road, depends on two factors:

- The type of road
- The type of vehicle you're driving

In Lesson 12, we described a dual carriageway as having two carriageways, and said that the speed limit on them is generally the same as on a motorway, 70mph, unless there are signs telling you otherwise.

A single carriageway – in other words, a standard country road – has a sixty limit. So, if you drive along an 'A' road up to the point where it changes from a *single* to a *dual* carriageway, there's also a change of speed limit, from sixty up to seventy. But there aren't any speed limit signs to let you know that, it's all about the change of road type.

And the type of vehicle is the other factor on national speed limit roads. Vans, trucks and cars-towing-trailers all have their own speed restrictions. So, if a big lorry's holding you up, plodding along at forty in a *sixty* – well, perhaps it's a 60mph limit for you, but not for them. For them it's either a forty or a fifty, depending on which side of Hadrian's Wall they're on!

On test, your Examiner expects you to drive at a **realistic** speed and to make **safe progress**. Essentially that means driving at-or-around the speed limit, unless there's a reason for driving any slower.

Oh, and Examiners like acceleration. Nothing too crazy, but acceleration shows confidence and control. Examiners don't like speeding, though. Speeding's illegal. You might get away with being, say, 10% over the limit for a short period, but don't bank on it. Some Examiners are stricter on this than others.

The majority of drivers, let's say 98%, drive their cars as if they were the carriages of a train, taking their time, merrily following the guy in front. That should be you. So, not one of the 1% creeping around the place, holding everyone else up, or like the other 1%, the dreaded *boy racers*. No – in driving, if not in life – just follow the crowd!

Anyway...now that we've got you all excited with all this talk of bombing along at sixty, let's calm things down again, and let's make sure that you're in the correct part of the road. Let's talk about...

Road Positioning

We drive on the left. But you're also expected to *keep over* to the left. So, on a nice wide main road, it's not acceptable to be virtually skimming the centre white line. Your general driving position is expected to be about a metre-or-so from the left side of the road, however wide it is. Though, of course, as we've now discussed many times in previous lessons, the General Rule does allow you to move to the right to overtake or to turn right.

When you're driving in lanes, aim to stay in the centre of your lane. That includes slip lanes and those right-turn lanes where you're protected from passing traffic by the hatched road markings.

On narrow country roads, you're expected to be far enough over to the left that when a car comes the other way you don't have to move over to the left to get out of its way. You should already be out of its way.

And, on those country roads, where you're skimming along past hedges, it can be tempting to improve your view around left-hand bends by moving out slightly to the right, towards the middle of the road. But, again, it's probably best to keep well over to the left.

And those hedge-lined left-hand bends are a nightmare. You can't see around them. The thing is, as drivers, we can really only deal with one problem at a time. So, on a bend, meeting a pedestrian unexpectedly halfway round, we can cope with that, we can steer out past.

But it's when we meet **two** problems that we're in trouble. So that pedestrian **plus** a tractor that's coming the other way. Now…if you're going in any way quick at this point, you're in real trouble. I'm afraid those cat-like reactions of yours aren't going to be enough to save the day.

So, on country roads, base your speed not only on what you can see, but also on how far you can see. And, if you're rounding a bend or cresting a hill – somewhere where you really can't see any further ahead than just a few car lengths – ask yourself: *what can't I see yet?*

But what if you *can* see something up ahead? Something slow. What if you're thinking about…

Overtaking

Overtaking anything is serious business and needs serious thought. So don't overtake at junctions or bends or the brows of hills, or outside petrol stations or schools. And only overtake if it's going to benefit your journey time – so don't overtake anything when you're two minutes from journey's end.

*

Parked cars on country roads are comparatively rare. So, as discussed way back in Lesson 8, unlike in thirty limits, it's best to indicate before moving out to pass them, especially if there's another car behind you.

Pedestrians, though, unlike parked cars, are actually fairly common on country roads. After all, there are very few footpaths. And, as we've already said, left-hand bends, especially when they have an overgrown hedge lining the road, are really dangerous, especially when it comes to meeting pedestrians because you just don't see them until the last moment.

When you do meet a pedestrian, indicate before pulling out to pass them. Pedestrians ahead of you might be difficult for following drivers to see, so your indicator could be the first warning those following drivers get that there's a problem up ahead.

And as for the pedestrians themselves, walking nervously towards you, imagine the relief they feel on seeing your indicator flashing away, letting them know that, not only have you seen them, but that you have the situation under control.

And cyclists need special consideration, too…

On any type of road, town or country, indicate past anything that's moving, including cyclists. Check your mirrors – to make sure there isn't some speedy guy already overtaking *you* – indicate, then give the cyclist plenty of room, a couple of metres at least, as you pass them. Finally, check your mirrors again before pulling back in, just to make sure you haven't left the poor cyclist lying in a heap on the ground!

And you need to do all that without inconveniencing any traffic coming in the other direction. So don't think: *hey, it's **only** a cyclist* and just fire on past…

So, if you can't overtake safely yet, follow the cyclist at a safe distance, a couple of car lengths back – close enough that you're ready to overtake when the opportunity arises, but not so close that you'll run into them if they stop. Be patient. As a learner driver yourself, you should know that it's always the slowest vehicle that dictates the speed of the traffic!

And overtaking cars? Well, on test that's fairly unlikely unless you're on a dual carriageway, which we covered in Lesson 12.

Okay, so who wants to go shopping? Good. Because we're off to the city centre…

CITY CENTRES

Lesson 14

Now, some of the things we'll be discussing here are potentially more like *advanced* driving than 'L' driving because of the way the driving test is evolving…

You see, back in the day, you were expected to drive on your test like the proverbial granny. Twenty-seven miles-per-hour, handbrake on at even the slightest pause, and your white-knuckle hands glued to the wheel at ten-to-two. Then, after your test, your family *elder* would take you out in their car and teach you how to *really* drive.

But then, as traffic got heavier and road systems more complicated, the test started to change. The use of your car's controls became more personal preference than do-as-I-say rules and **safe progress** became a thing.

- *Safe:* keep it legal, don't upset anyone, don't crash
- *Progress*: get from A-to-B in a timely manner

And nowhere has this been more noticeable than in our busiest towns and cities. Driving techniques that would've been unthinkable a generation ago are now necessary, even on a test. In fact, if you're too cautious, it's not unknown for an Examiner to *gently* suggest what they think would be your best course of action!

But let's not get ahead of ourselves here – we're not talking *boy racer* – but when you pass your test nowadays, you know you've earned it, you know you can cope with modern traffic, and you know you can already *really* drive.

Busy traffic is like a game of chess. The pieces move in different ways to different rules at different beats. Each piece has strengths and weaknesses, each moves easily, keeping the game flowing.

For drivers, keeping that flow is all about knowing the correct lane to be in – and being in it nice-n-early. It's the key to a stress-free city-life. But maybe you're a stranger in town – the test routes new to you – so maybe it's not that easy.

If that's the case, take your time. Direction signs can be lost in the sea of glass and neon, but they are there. So look even further ahead than normal, especially when you're stationary, and search them out.

Remember that busy routes are often one-way systems, and that on a one-way system traffic can be passing you on either side. There's no overtaking lane on a one-way street.

And then, whether you're new to this town or a regular, get used to sharing. Sharing road space, sharing time. Sometimes other drivers wait for you; sometimes you wait for other drivers. Sit back and let things sort themselves out in front of you. Let other drivers do their thing. You can't hurry them.

But, even if you're chilled out, heavy traffic can still feel overwhelming. Lots of lanes, lots of metal. If you feel your stress levels rising, try to focus on your immediate area. Focus on your lane, keeping to the centre of it, keeping well back from the car in front. I mean, no matter how heavy the traffic, no matter how many lanes there are, it's really only the car directly ahead of you that's your immediate concern.

Now, to keep your car moving smoothly in heavy traffic, picture a boy kicking his football along the pavement alongside you. He gives it a little kick and the ball rolls…then another little kick.

You do a similar thing with your car. Ease the clutch up and give the car a little kick with the engine. Then, when the brake lights ahead of you flash on again, press your clutch down and coast. Let your car roll for a bit. Maybe you need the brake, maybe you don't. Then clutch up again…another kick. There's nothing wrong with using controlled coasting. There's nothing wrong with pressing the clutch down before the brake when you're in first gear.

And there's nothing wrong with…

Changing Lanes

When you're changing lanes, give-way to the traffic already in the lane you want to move into. But just like emerging from a side street, that doesn't mean you have to wait for someone to *let you in*. No, moving over is fine, provided you don't inconvenience drivers in that lane, you don't force them to brake or swerve.

Think of those lane lines, separating the lanes, as if they were kerb stones rather than just paint. It is usually possible to mount a kerb in your car but you must do it carefully and thoughtfully – not clumsily and rushed – because otherwise you will end up damaging your car. Changing lanes is the same…

So, check your mirrors, pop an indicator on, a quick blind-spot glance, then ease over towards the white line, just to let the other drivers know you want to move across. This is a driver's version of assertive body language: you're being positive without being aggressive.

When you're being positive in this way, other drivers will be more likely to let you in. But if you're too timid and shying away from the white line, or too aggressive and veering across onto it,

159

then you've got no chance. The traffic will close up and you'll be ignored.

When changing lanes, try to avoid making snap decisions. Use those door mirrors. Use those blind-spot checks. Sometimes it's better to let the lane-change pass you by rather than make a rash move.

It's the same when you're trying to move away in heavy traffic. Normally indicators are used to tell other folk what you're planning on doing, but sometimes – when traffic's flowing past you like a river – you can use a *begging signal*, where you just stick an indicator on and watch your door mirror for some kind soul to let you in. Sometimes it's the only way you're going to get out.

Turning into side streets can also be a problem, especially if you have to cross either a bus or a cycle lane. Watch out for cyclists whizzing up on your left, or even threading between lanes of cars.

Anyway, in heavy traffic, if you're having trouble changing lanes or pulling out of a side street, you could do worse than try a couple of the…

Tricks Of The Trade

…used by crafty old lorry-drivers!

First, try and seek out eye-contact with passing drivers. A truck driver, stuck in a side road, will wind their window down and look directly at the drivers in that passing queue of cars, from the cab of their big, slow lorry. Of course, the car drivers don't want to let the lorry in, they don't want to be stuck behind it, so they'll pretend not to have noticed. But, eventually, the lorry driver will catch a car driver's eye, and that reluctant driver will let the lorry in. Works every time.

You see, traffic's an impersonal thing, everyone in their own metal box, their own suit of armour. But if you establish eye contact with a fellow driver, that armour's stripped away. You become just two people again. Two human beings.

Another technique, to help you get out of a busy side street, is to look for gaps in traffic rather than just at the traffic itself. We touched on this in Lesson 11, talking about getting onto a roundabout, and this maybe sounds obvious, but it's easy to fall into the trap of just watching the traffic flowing past you...

So, remember to watch both sides of the street – especially when turning right – keep your head swivelling from side to side. Say to yourself: *there's a gap after the blue car to the left...there's a gap after the red van to the right*, and when those two gaps coincide... you're off.

Don't just stare at traffic, say, from your right until there's a gap then look to your left. You might have just missed a chance to go, and, if not, by the time you're mentally up-to-speed again with the traffic coming from your left, the situation from your right will have changed. So, imagine you're watching tennis – Wimbledon – your head turning rhythmically, left to right, keeping score!

Sometimes your view's going to be blocked by, say, a parked delivery van or a bus. When this happens, there's no point sitting at the give-way line, unable to see a thing. You're going to have to use that *creep-n-peep* technique. Creeping forward, super carefully, using the clutch, so that you can peep around whatever's blocking your view...

Think of the give way line as bending out, moulding itself around that van, with you going out to it, edging the car forward while leaning your body forward, but not committing yourself to finally going until you can see around the van, you can see that the road's clear.

As you creep-n-peep, you can use reflections from car bodywork or shop windows to help you catch a glimpse of movement from approaching traffic. Sometimes you'll catch sight of movement from shadows or from feet moving beneath vans or buses.

Watching for feet can help you spot children getting off a school bus then crossing in front of it, or van drivers checking their notes as they walk out around their vans – *right there* – in front of you.

Another creeping forward technique, that might help you emerge from a side-street onto a traffic-packed city street – again, when you're turning right – is to move forward into the middle of the road, when you have a gap from the right, but then to wait out there in the middle, either for a gap in traffic from the left or for a kind driver to let you out. So you're effectively using the line running along the centre of the major road as a kind of give-way line.

Oh, and another trick – this one for busy roundabouts – is to use busses and other long vehicles as a **shield** when you're emerging. If you're waiting at a roundabout and there's a bus to your right, when it moves off you can go with it. Nothing's going to come *through* the bus! So, as long as you keep up with it as it pulls away, you'll be fine…

A word of caution, though. This trick doesn't work with those big 4x4s. They're tall, yes, but not long enough – and way too fast – for this trick to work!

But what you can do to help against those tall cars – those 4x4s and the like – especially when you're emerging and turning left, is to sit back a little bit at junctions and look along the road from **behind** them…

With most cars, if they're alongside you, you can look **through** them. But not with those guys – not unless you're in one yourself. So hold back to get a view of the road, then, when you're clear, ease forward for a final check around the front of them before moving away.

Then, in the side streets, you'll see guys accelerating up to...

Speed Bumps

...then braking, going over them at walking pace, then accelerating again, up to the next one. This just puts unnecessary wear-n-tear on the brakes and tyres, and wastes fuel.

When you brake, the front of your car dips down slightly because the weight of the car is transferred forward, pressing down on the front suspension. If there's an apple on your back seat, and you brake, it'll fall on the floor. Now, braking at a speed bump causes the front of your car to squat down, using up some of the bounce in your suspension, making the bump feel much harsher than it really is.

So, when you meet a speed bump, ideally you want to be off the brakes, but travelling slowly enough to go over it smoothly. In fact, the best way of dealing with speed bumps is to *drive* over them, your engine gently pulling you over, with careful use of the accelerator.

The trick, for a nice smooth ride – and one that's just as quick from A-to-B – is to keep a steady speed along the length of the road, allowing your suspension to soak-up speed bumps, going easy on both the accelerator and the brakes in between.

In town, you've also got a whole bunch of...

Pedestrian Crossings

There are good old-fashioned *zebra crossings*, of course, though they're being phased out.

As are **pelican crossings**. These are traffic-light controlled pedestrian crossings where the lights work through a slightly different sequence to normal traffic lights.

They go…

- Green
- Amber
- Red
- Flashing amber
- Green

At pelican crossings, both the red and flashing amber phases last for around ten seconds. So as you approach the crossing you can literally countdown 10, 9, 8 and so on.

On the flashing-amber phase, the rule is to stop for any pedestrians who are actually crossing, even if they're not directly in front of you. You have to wait for the crossing to be completely clear before you move on. But you don't have to wait for the green light. You can go on the flashing amber, as long as the crossing's clear.

Puffin and **toucan** crossings are the newer designs. They use sensors mounted on top of the lights to *watch* folk using the crossing, then change accordingly. So it's harder to judge when they'll change back to green, though it seems to still generally be around ten-to-twelve seconds.

Puffin crossings are for pedestrians but toucan crossings are for both pedestrians and cyclists – which is why they're remembered by thinking **two** – as in the number two – can cross. **Two-can cross**.

On all traffic light crossings, and traffic lights in general, as you slow down approaching the back of a queue of traffic, don't start to accelerate the moment you see the lights up ahead changing to green. It takes a couple of seconds for each vehicle to react to the one in front of it moving. So, if there are ten stationary cars between you and the lights, it might take twenty seconds before the car directly in front of you starts to move. Think of the traffic moving away as being like a row of falling dominoes – one after another – and time your approach accordingly.

And have you noticed the **zigzag** lines painted either side of pedestrian crossings? They have two rules:

- No parking
- No overtaking the vehicle nearest the crossing

If you're approaching a pedestrian crossing on, say, a two-lane one-way street,   and the crossing seems to be clear, it's tempting to overtake a row of vehicles sitting there, stationary, in the other lane.

But what if the reason they're sitting there is because of **one last pedestrian** who's now crossing in front of the traffic? And what if the vehicle at the head of the queue is a van, a van big enough to block your view of that **one last pedestrian** until they pop out, right *there* in front of you?

I *kind of* have personal experience of this. When I was a baby, my Mum, pushing me up to a zebra crossing in my pram, was waved across the road by the driver of a big red London bus, only for the bus to then be overtaken by the driver of a big black London taxi – which hit the pram and spilled me out across the street. Not great.

Your Examiner will get nervous if you get too close to any pedestrians during your test, so give pedestrians plenty of room and slow down if they're crossing in front of you.

But remember that *The Highway Code* says to not actually wave pedestrians across the road. The danger is that the pedestrian might think that the *traffic* has stopped. But you're not *the* traffic, not all of it, you're just one car, but – especially children – don't think of it like that. So don't wave them across the road but then expect them to look in the other direction. Chances are they won't.

Finally, watch for pedestrians walking between stationary cars. Your lane might be moving, but if the lane alongside you isn't, pedestrians will come marching through, possibly still focused on their phones.

In busy traffic, then, probably more so than anywhere else, take your time, use your judgement, and try to make safe progress.

*

And that's pretty much it for the normal-driving phase of your lessons. If you've been able to practise these lessons then hopefully you're now starting to develop good car control, and you have a good understanding of how the road works: so driving in residential areas and busy towns, on dual carriageways and in the countryside, and also how to deal with the different types of complex junctions, like traffic lights and roundabouts…

Now we move on to Section 3, as it's time for you to start thinking about your practical driving test.

So, let's head on over to the Driving Test Centre and say *hello* to your Driving Examiner…

YOUR DRIVING EXAMINER

Lesson 15

When adult conversation turns to *driving*, the question always asked is, *did you pass first time?*

In years to come, when you're asked that question, you want the answer to be a resounding *YES!*

If life were a Hollywood movie then passing your driving test would be the great coming of age story – like a first love or a rite-of-passage – because, although most adults drive, most don't pass first time. And there's always drama...

And this drama stems from the stress of it all, along with the fine margins between a pass and a fail. It's not easy.

The driving test's pass rate has always sat at a national average of just over 40%. So, if a driving examiner does a normal day's work of seven tests, on average, three pass, four fail.

So why so many fails?

One reason is that, no matter how well prepared your Supervisor considers you to be, there's a fair chance the test still seems a complete mystery to you. Every Driving Instructor will tell you that, **oh well, at least now I know what to expect next time** is the most often heard phrase uttered by learner drivers on the sad drive home after a failed test.

But it doesn't have to be that way. There's nothing complicated about the driving test. Yes, it's evolved over the years, but it's still essentially the same test as it was when it began, seventy-odd years ago. It's the same test your grandparents took.

So the driving test is an open book. This book. And, as we move into Section 3, we'll be discussing what you can expect from the test, what you can expect from your Examiner, and what your Examiner will expect from you.

We'll go through the component parts of a driving test: from the marking system and how your Examiner will give you directions, to the manoeuvres and exercises you'll be asked to complete. And we'll look at the main reasons for test fails – and how to avoid them.

Anyway, let's dive in with a question…

What Do I Have To Do To Pass?

Good question. And I'm not being funny here, but the answer is: *don't fail*.

Look, I know it sounds weird but it's true: you begin your practical driving test with a pass. That's right: you don't actually have to **pass** the driving test. No, what you really have to do is to **not fail it!** Your Driving Examiner starts the test with a clear screen on their tablet – **zero faults** – and their job is to then make a note of any mistakes you might make, **not** to make notes on the stuff you do well.

So…wait. Hang on. You start the driving test with a pass?

Yep. You sure do. Your Examiner – and the whole-entire Government, for that matter – wants you to pass.

Sounds crazy? Maybe, but see, as a driver you'll become the ultimate tax payer. When you drive, you'll pay tax on your car and its insurance, you'll pay tax on its spares and repairs, and you'll pay a huge amount of tax on the fuel you pump in and the emissions it pumps out. You'll pay tax just to be allowed to use the road. What, you think you own your car just because you buy it with your own hard-earned money? No, you will be the *keeper* of that car. I mean, just try leaving an untaxed car out on the street to see who really owns it! You'll be waving bye-bye to your pride-n-joy in no time!

So, your Examiner's job is simply to confirm what you and your Supervisor hopefully already know: that you can drive legally and safely, and all on your own – all without instruction.

But if, in your Examiner's opinion, you do something illegal or unsafe, or they feel you still need some help with your driving, then you're not considered ready to drive on your own just yet, so you're sent away to try again another day.

Your Examiner's *opinion*… Driving Examiners are like referees. All sports have rules, and referees are given guidelines on how to interpret those rules, but whether-or-not a potential foul becomes a penalty is down to the referee's opinion.

But it can't be a *kind of* penalty. It either is or it isn't.

It's the same on your driving test. Unlike, say, a history essay, there are no 'B' or 'C' grades on a driving test. It's either 'A' or 'F'. It's either pass or fail.

And remember, your Examiner marks down the mistakes you make, the *faults*. They don't officially note down the good stuff during your drive, the things you do well.

Ah…but even though they don't *officially* note what you do well – contrary to popular opinion – they are human, so they are impressionable. And, in us humans, good impressions can go a long way.

So, a driving test candidate who's driven really well, right up to the point where they – *oh no* – make a mistake, is more likely to be given the benefit of the doubt than one who's been looking a bit dodgy from the very beginning.

So, make sure you're well prepared for your test, drive to make a good impression, and you'll sail through…

And that's with whichever Examiner you get! Because some, unfortunately, can get a bit of a bad reputation! I suppose, like in all professions, some are just friendlier than others. Some go out of their way to calm your nerves, while others seem to add to them, huffing at your every mistake.

But, if you do get the Examiner that all your friends have told you is a *total nightmare*, don't take that Examiner's huffing, or whatever, personally, because – and here's the thing – **all the Examiners have the same pass rate**.

Yep, the friendly one, the one you were hoping to get, fails just as many folk as the *old moan* you've ended up with! So, to turn that on its head, *your* Examiner passes just as many candidates as the *nice* one.

You see, any Examiner whose pass rate is noticeably different from his colleagues will receive a visit from his boss to see what the *problem* is. Now, personally, if I were an Examiner, I'd want to avoid those nasty visits, so I'd make pretty sure my pass rate was roughly the same as everyone else's.

So, ignore your Examiner.

And that includes when they start tapping at their tablets…

Part of their job is to keep a record of the tasks you've completed, so when they tap away they're not necessarily marking a fault against you, they have plenty of other things to think about.

And so do you…

Your focus should be on driving as well as you possibly can, not on what your Examiner's doing.

Okay, so to sum up so far: Examiners are referees, trained to follow a rule book, but they're not machines – they have opinions, they make judgements, and they're all different. And the test itself is negatively marked, which means you begin your test with a pass, which in turn means that your job is simply to make sure that you don't fail.

So, *the system* – here at least – is on your side.

But not everybody passes first time…

As we've already seen, if an Examiner typically sees seven test candidates in a day, on average, three pass but four fail. Now, of the four who fail, statistically, one either isn't yet ready for the test or else just makes a one-off mistake. Happens to the best of us.

Or maybe they were just unlucky…

Unlucky in that, if you were to, say, forget a blind spot glance when lane changing, but there's nobody there – in your blind spot – then your Examiner might not consider it to be that big a deal; but if there *is* another vehicle alongside you then that same mistake could now easily become a test fail.

Or perhaps you're just about to emerge from a side road… You've looked carefully, both ways, multiple times, you're sure it's safe, so you start to pull out – when your Examiner shouts STOP – as a speeding lunatic comes flying past you.

Nightmare.

Your Examiner knows the other guy was speeding, but they also know they had to step in to stop you to avoid a crash… So you fail your test. I know maybe that doesn't sound fair, but that's the way this particular cookie crumbles…

Anyway, of the other three failures: one fails in relation to *priority* – so not *giving way* correctly. One fails because they aren't using their mirrors properly or checking those blind spots. And one fails during their reversing manoeuvre, usually in relation to observation.

So don't make it easy for your Examiner to fail you. Get back to basics, and get those basics right:

- Moving away procedure
- Junctions and priority
- Mirrors and blind spots
- Manoeuvres

The reversing exercise – **your manoeuvre** – is responsible for around 25% of fails, which is huge considering it'll only take-up about 5% of the time you'll spend with your Examiner! So all the manoeuvres are super-important and we'll be getting into them in detail soon.

But for now, let's end this part of the lesson with two thoughts…

The first is that your driving test is an exercise in concentration, an exercise in *mindfulness.* I know, I know…but the point is this, don't allow yourself to be distracted by thoughts of what's already happened or what might be about to happen further along the line. Focus on what you're doing now and on planning for the immediate future.

The level of concentration needed here is similar to that required to do a basic mental arithmetic test. So, nothing particularly difficult – addition and subtraction, a few *times tables* – but here's the thing: although this test only lasts about thirty-five minutes you're not allowed to get any *questions* wrong…

Remember, it's pass or fail – there are no 'B' grades!

So, concentrate on what you're doing, every step of the way…

Think of someone – anyone – who's just arrived in Florida for a fly-drive holiday. There they are, driving on the *wrong* side of the car and on the *wrong* side of the road, totally out of their comfort zone. Then, as they catch sight of that first set of traffic lights, the ones as you leave the airport, they cry out, "What the $&%£ are you supposed to do here?!"

Well, try not to swear, but that's the level of focus you must bring to every junction on your test. Take nothing for granted. Don't assume things will just happen as they should. Mirror, signal, speed and gear. Think things through. *What should I do here?*

Okay, so I mentioned two thoughts, the second one is speed. Examiners are in no hurry.

Take your time.

Warning: I'm about to make up a statistic here and pass it off as fact. Like a politician…

Here goes: you are one hundred times more likely to fail your test for driving too quickly than you are for driving too slowly.

Examiners are quick to fail people who are too quick, slow to fail people who are too slow.

You don't have to impress your Examiner into passing you – you start with a pass – no, you must *bore* your Examiner into not failing you! No drama. Drive like you're taking Granny to church, not like you're late for work.

Take your time!

Now, that doesn't mean that you should be driving at 10mph below the speed limit everywhere, or that you should stop and put the handbrake on at every roundabout – whether it's clear or not – but it means that where there's a balance to be struck between fast or slow – *should I stay or should I go* – then err on the side of caution. And stay.

But not too cautious! Remember, *safe progress*. So use the speed limit where it's safe, and keep moving at give-way junctions when you're absolutely certain it's safe to go. Use your judgement. Trust yourself. But if you're torn between whether-or-not you should pull out…then wait.

Take your time!

Anyway, let's further discuss this mythical creature known only as…

Your Driving Examiner

On test day, you waiting nervously in the test-centre waiting-room, the door to the back office squeaks open and in marches your Driving Examiner, dressed in a trendy fluorescent yellow sleeveless number.

Now, as far as we're concerned, your Examiner has two jobs:

- To make a note of any mistakes you might make
- To direct you around your driving test route

So, let's talk about the way your Examiner uses…

The Marking System

Your Examiner has a pre-printed **learn to drive** list in front of them as you start your test. Everything from how you use the individual controls of the car right through to how you deal with junctions and other traffic. It's a pretty long list! It's a comprehensive list of everything you've been through in this book or on your driving lessons.

However, don't let yourself get too hung up on thinking about that list. Instead, think of it as a clean sheet of crisp white paper, pure as the driven snow, your Examiner simply noting down any mistakes you make. Then think of yourself driving so carefully and so well that your Examiner has nothing to write about!

Oh, and as you probably remember, mistakes on a driving test are known as *faults*.

There are three levels of fault that your Examiner can mark against you. The most serious is a *dangerous* fault. That's one where they have to take action to avoid either an accident or a potentially dangerous situation. They can take either verbal or physical action. So, perhaps you're given a quick verbal warning – *mind that bike!* – or perhaps your Examiner takes control of the car by either steering or using the handbrake, or, if the car has dual controls, by using those.

Dangerous faults are a fail. You're not allowed any of those.

Next down on the scale are *serious* faults. Like dangerous faults, these are the ones you'll often hear being referred to as *major* faults.

Just one serious fault is also a test fail.

So, as far as we're concerned, both dangerous and serious faults are essentially the same thing. You're not allowed any of either of them.

Finally, there are *driving* faults. These used to be known, back-in-the-day, as *minor* faults. So, slight mistakes.

Maybe you forgot to check your mirror back there before indicating, or maybe your blind spot check before moving away on your hill-start was a bit too casual for your Examiner's liking. Whatever, these are the kind of things that are generally scored against you as driving faults.

At the end of the test the driving faults are added up. You're allowed up to **fifteen** of them. So, if you get a sixteenth one, even if you don't have any dangerous or serious faults, it's still a fail. But to score sixteen faults you'd have to be getting a driving fault, so making a noticeable mistake, every couple of minutes, which probably means you're not yet ready to drive on your own anyway.

But there's another way you can fail the test through your driving faults, and that's if you keep on making exactly the same mistake. So, no…stalling the engine isn't necessarily a serious fault, provided you make the car safe before re-starting. But if you keep on stalling…three…four times, then your Examiner's likely to decide that you need more practise, so they're likely to upgrade those driving faults into a serious fault.

So, to recap, there are four ways you can fail the test:

- One-or- more dangerous faults
- One-or-more serious faults
- Sixteen-or-more driving faults
- Or a pattern of committing the same driving fault several times

Take your time…

Examiners are *quick to fail people who are too quick but slow to fail people who are too slow*…

The point is that faults relating to being too quick or too impulsive are likely to be marked as *serious*, while faults relating to being too slow or too cautious are likely to be marked as *driving* – so *minor* – faults.

So that's faults. Now let's talk about the way Examiners instruct you on test, and how they give…

Route Directions

At the beginning of your test, once you've got yourself settled into your car, your Examiner starts the drive by saying something like: *I'd like you to follow the road ahead, unless road markings or traffic signs direct you otherwise. If I want you to turn either left or right I'll tell you in good time.*

Then they ask if you understand, to which, hopefully, you'll say yes, then they'll tell you to, *move on when you're ready, please.*

So your Examiner directs you in a similar way to a sat-nav. Sat-navs say, *follow the course of the road.* Examiners say, *follow the road ahead.* It's the same thing.

Roundabouts and traffic lights are similar too...

At roundabouts a sat-nav will tell you which exit to take, even if that exit goes straight-ahead. Your Examiner does the same. And at traffic lights, both your Examiner and your sat-nav only speak to you if they want you to turn. They don't keep on saying, *go straight on.*

So, to recap: at any given junction, if your Examiner stays quiet, it's because they want you to follow the road ahead. Except at roundabouts – at roundabouts they'll always direct you, whichever direction they want you to take. But, at other junctions, including traffic-lights, if they want you to follow the road ahead, they simply stay quiet.

Following the road ahead sounds pretty straightforward. But, although we drive on the left, it isn't always the left-hand lane that goes straight-ahead. Sometimes arrows tell you to use the centre or the right-hand lane. And, in traffic, often you just follow the car up ahead.

But not always.

Sometimes you have to leave the safety of the queue to go your own way. So, following the road ahead isn't as easy as it sounds. It requires awareness and planning. Your Examiner won't tell you which lane to use. You're expected to sort out lanes and junctions for yourself, to *read* the road.

So, to practise reading the road, it's really important to practise following the road ahead. You need to be able to sort out complex junctions for yourself. Because, on test, faced with a silent Examiner, you're going to struggle if you're used to someone constantly directing you, constantly instructing you, and constantly telling you to *go straight on.*

Something else you'll need to practise for your test is called…

Independent Driving

This is when, rather than your Examiner directing you junction-by-junction, they often reach for their sat-nav and get it fired-up with a pre-planned route of around twenty minutes driving time. Then you're left to follow the directions from the sat-nav, rather than from the Examiner.

An alternative is you being given a short series of directions to follow – often while being shown a basic diagram depicting the route (with you parked at the side of the road, of course!)…

Something like, **at the next three traffic-light junctions I'd like you to turn left**.

Or you might be asked to follow direction signs for a particular destination…

So, *I'd like you to start following signs for London.*

The two main things to note about independent driving are that, number one, if at any time you're confused by something your Examiner's said, or you're unsure of where you should be going, then you can ask your Examiner for clarification. You're not penalised for having a rubbish sense of direction! But, as our American friends might say, try to ask for help *ahead of time.* So, approaching a roundabout, for example, if you don't know where you're supposed to be going, ask before you get there!

And, number two. If you do make a mistake, so if you find yourself, say, in the wrong lane at a roundabout, or you realise that you're in the process of turning left when you should be turning right… well, again, try not to panic. Because, provided you stay calm and stay safe, you won't be marked down. So, continue with the turn – even though you think you've messed up – and wait for your poor old Examiner to re-direct you back onto the correct route.

But, whatever you do, if you find yourself in that situation, don't try to make last-ditch lane-changes or turns. That would be potentially dangerous, so **that** would be a fail.

Then, at the end of the independent drive, your Examiner will say: **that's the end of your independent drive. Now I'll just direct you as normal.** Then, true to their word, they'll start directing you junction-by-junction again. Though, of course, they'll stay quiet if they just want you to follow the road ahead.

And they'll also stay quiet if you start making…

Silly Mistakes

Now, as we discussed earlier in this lesson, most test fails come down to one of the usual suspects: priority, mirrors, manoeuvres…

So…*driving* in other words! The basics. Getting the basics right is absolutely crucial to driving safely and so to passing your test.

Don't try to kid yourself that making mistakes with these fundamentals are just *silly* mistakes.

As an instructor, it's common, after talking someone through a mistake-or-two, that they've perhaps just made on a roundabout, to have them end the conversation with a breezy, *so just a couple of silly mistakes then*, as though it's not really a problem.

But how should we define a *silly mistake?* Well, dump the word *silly* but keep the word **mistake!** Because, harsh as it may seem, just one *silly* mistake could be enough for your Examiner to fail you.

It's easy to convince yourself that the silly mistakes only happen because this is *just* a lesson or *just* a practise drive and it won't happen on your test. But that's not the case. If you still find yourself making silly mistakes on your lessons then you'll definitely get found out on your test.

You don't have to be perfect to pass the test, but you do have to be able to drive legally and safely and on your own.

But for now, let's go over a bit of revision, and begin at the beginning with…

Moving Away Safely

I'd like you pull over on the left, when it's safe to do so, please.

You'll be hearing that a lot on test. Examiners love it. Getting you to pull over then to move away again.

Okay, three things.

One: don't say to your Examiner – **what, anywhere?** – when you're asked to pull over. They won't say **yes**. Instead, you'll get a confusing reply along the lines of, **do what your Supervisor taught you to do**. Because, your Examiner isn't only watching **how** you park, they're also watching **where** you park. So choosing where to stop is very much a part of the test.

So don't park at a bus stop or over some guy's driveway. Don't park near the brow of a hill or on a bend. Don't park opposite a side road. Don't park where it says *no parking*.

And two: some Examiners might use language that's a bit more chilled than the *official* wording. **Find us a nice spot to pull over along here, please.** That kind of thing.

But, same as for any other aspect of the test, if you're not sure of something, you're allowed to ask. Your Examiner won't mind.

Finally, three: slow down. Take your time. If the road ahead of you is completely clear of parked cars then just ease carefully over to the kerb and stop in the gear that you're already in – there's probably no need to change down. But if the road's lined with parked cars, slow down and change down into 2nd, keeping yourself parallel with the parked cars – not drifting in towards them – while looking for a suitable place to stop.

So the full procedure would be:

- Mirrors
- Indicate left
- Slow down and, if necessary, change down
- Then pull up along the kerb
- Handbrake and neutral
- Cancel your indicator

Try to find a reference point on your car that you can use when you're pulling over. Maybe you can line the kerb up with a point along the bottom of your windscreen. But try not to stare into your left-hand door mirror as you come into the kerb. If you're at an angle, then the back of your car will be further from the kerb than the front, so you'll get a false impression if you only use the door mirror.

Anyway, try to get your car around six inches from the kerb. But try not to hit it! A slight scuff will probably only be a minor driving fault but a good whack could be a fail.

Then, when you're asked to move away again, remember to complete your moving away sequence *before* releasing the handbrake:

- Clutch in
- First gear

- Set the gas (liven up the engine a bit)
- Clutch up to *the bite*
- Mirror
- Indicate
- (grab hold of the handbrake)
- Blind spot
- Door mirror

Only then, once you've completed everything on that list, do you finally release the handbrake and move away.

Oh, and that's everything on that list ***in the correct order***…

Don't indicate before you've even put the car in gear. What would happen if someone flashed their lights to let you out? Chances are, in your rush to get going, you'd end up stalling.

And note where the blind spot check comes in. There's no point doing it at the beginning of your sequence – things change, cars turn out of side streets – it should be done **just before** you finally move away.

Now, when it comes to the signal to move away, ideally you only indicate when you can see in your mirrors that it's safe for you to move away, that you're not going to inconvenience any traffic coming up behind you. So the signal is primarily to warn folk in front of you that you're about to start heading towards them!

But remember, sometimes, in really-heavy slow-moving traffic, it's necessary to use a ***begging*** signal – putting one on in the hope of getting somebody to let you out. Then, when someone *does* let you out, don't forget to smile and wave to say *thanks.*

On test, there will also be a couple of times when your Examiner will ask you to pull over in order to watch you demonstrating specific skills when you move away again…

The Hill Start And The Angled Start.

On the **hill start**, when you move away, try not to either stall or roll back. So, if you're driving a manual car, you'll need to liven up the engine a bit more than on a level road.

And if this manual car is front-wheel drive, and most are, you'll also need to lift the clutch up to the point where the bonnet rises up a fraction. The *holding point.* That extra power will help prevent your engine from stalling, and the holding point will prevent you from rolling back.

Then, when you release the handbrake, try to initially keep both feet still for a couple of seconds before easing the clutch up fully. Avoid lifting the clutch abruptly.

For the **angled start**, you'll be asked to pull over ***close to the car up ahead.*** Stop, neat to the kerb, so that you can just see the road surface between you and that car. Then, when you move away again, steer quickly, while keeping your car moving slowly, keeping it under control with the clutch.

The important thing with the angled start, though, is to give-way – not just to traffic coming up behind you – but to oncoming traffic as well, because as you move out to pass the car in front, you're going to be moving out onto the wrong side of the road.

So take your time.

*

And with that sound advice – ***take your time*** – ringing in your ears, we move on to the first of the set piece exercises you'll be asked to complete…

THE EMERGENCY STOP

Lesson 16

At some point during your test, your Examiner will ask you to pull over at the side of the road. Then, when you're parked, they'll say: *shortly I'll ask you stop as though in an emergency, as though a child has run out in front of you. When I give you the signal, I want you to stop the car quickly but under control.*

The signal, by the way, is them raising their right hand and saying: *Stop!*

Now, before you move away again, make sure you're completely clear in your mirrors. If there's anything following you, your Examiner won't ask you to do the emergency stop. Instead, they'll probably just get you to pull over again, to let any traffic pass, before trying it all over again.

So, nice clear mirrors and move away. Then drive *normally.* I know that sounds obvious but some people either go really slowly – as though that'll give them some kind of advantage – or else they take off like a rally driver, on a wave of emergency-stop-fuelled adrenaline.

So, accelerate and change-up normally. Then deal with any problems that might arise normally, too. You're not going to be asked to do this halfway past a bin lorry or a school bus. So, if you meet a hazard, slow down and deal with it in the normal way.

Anyway, once you're on the move, your Examiner will prepare to give you the signal. You'll be in 2nd or 3rd gear – or maybe the signal will come during the actual gear change – and you'll be doing around 20-30mph. They'll check that there's nothing behind you, and that you're not going to cause any problems for anybody up ahead of you, either...

Then you'll get the signal: *Stop!*

Okay, so now your Examiner wants to see six things:

- A fast reaction to their signal
- Quick, progressive braking
- Footbrake *then* clutch
- Hands on the wheel until you've stopped
- Secure the car
- Full observation before moving away again

Let's add in some detail.

When you're given the signal, you're expected to react quickly, to move your foot immediately to the brake – after all, **a child has run out** – so, no, you don't need to check your mirrors first!

Then brake **progressively**. Try saying to yourself the word *push* as you brake. Or counting out *one, two, three*. What you're trying to do is prevent yourself from just stamping down on the pedal. You're trying to stop the car quickly – ideally within a couple of car lengths – but without needing the car's Antilock Braking System, its ABS, to help you control it, especially on a nice dry road.

Now, having said that, assuming your car does have ABS, it's okay if you do brake aggressively enough to trigger the ABS – especially if the road's wet or slippery – but, as I said, if the road's dry, you shouldn't need it. Oh, and if you do use the ABS you'll know because you'll feel the brake pedal vibrate against the sole of your foot, and in some cars the hazard lights will come on too.

The level of braking needed will be just a little bit more urgent than if you've been caught-out by a traffic-light turning red. Nothing too crazy. When you practise, start fairly gently, increasing your pressure on the brakes as your confidence grows.

Once you're on the brakes it's time to get the clutch down, all the while keeping your hands up on the wheel. So it's brakes then clutch. Try not to do both together, and definitely don't go clutch first.

The reason for this technique is that, if you go for both feet together but accidentally get the clutch down a split-second before the brake then, especially if you're travelling downhill, your car will take a little – but possibly crucial – bit longer to stop.

When you've stopped, put the handbrake on and shift into neutral. If the hazard lights have come on, switch them off.

Now *breathe.* Try to settle the adrenaline that'll be flowing through you.

Then your Examiner will say, *I won't ask you to do that again. Move on when you're ready, please.*

Now, before you move away again, say to yourself: *three, two, one.* That's:

- Three: All three mirrors
- Two: Both blind spots
- One: Back to the rear-view mirror

Try not to leave any of those safety checks out. You're expected to do them all. Then, if you can move away again safely, do so. But if there's a vehicle coming up behind you, and you don't think you can move away safely before it reaches you, just wait. Don't indicate. Don't move. Just wait. See what the other driver does. If they sit behind you, indicate right and move away again. If they pass, do your *three, two, one* again then drive away.

Now, let's rewind a bit. After you've stopped the car and you have it secured, note that your Examiner will say, **I won't ask you to do that again,** before saying, **move on when you're ready, please.**

So, why does your Examiner bother with, **I won't ask you to do that again**?

Well, imagine that, later on in the test, your Examiner's brother comes driving along towards you and, out of habit, your Examiner lifts his hand to wave at him… And you hit the brakes! Well, you can just imagine the potential carnage!

So, just like any other manoeuvre that you might be asked to carry-out on test, you do this once, and once only.

Anyway, that's it. *Easy-peasy*. The entire thing, start-to-finish, takes less than a minute. Your Examiner's watching to see what you do when you're put under pressure: testing your reaction and seeing how well you control the brakes.

Practise on dry roads and wet roads. Practise in both 2nd and 3rd gears. Practise while changing from 2nd to 3rd. And practise over a range of speeds.

And, if your car has ABS, practise using it by quickly pressing both the brake and the clutch fully down hard.

ABS is a fantastic safety feature. In an emergency it prevents your car from skidding, even when you've got that brake pressed hard down on a wet road. It does it by *pulsing* the brakes – on, off, on, off – at lightening speed. You see, the big problem with a skidding car is that you can't steer it. But with the ABS activated, you can still steer to avoid obstacles, even if you're panic braking.

But ABS is not some kind of magic trick. It's clever, but it's not *that* clever. At high speed on a wet road it won't stop you instantly. It can still only stop you using the grip your tyres have available. So, yes, ABS is great, but don't think that you can always rely on it to get you out of trouble.

And after your test, when you've been driving for a while, practise stopping from higher speeds. I mean, how many people do you know who are perfectly happy driving along at speeds from which they've never actually tried to stop?

And with that thought in mind, let's move onto the one part of the test that everybody dreads…

THE REVERSING MANOEUVRES

Lesson 17

First of all, you're not alone... ***Everybody*** dreads doing *their* manoeuvre!

At some point during your test, your Examiner will ask you to carry out an exercise that involves reversing. It'll only take you two-or-three minutes to complete, yet the reversing manoeuvre is responsible for a quarter of all test fails.

There are four:

- Reversing into a parking bay
- Parallel parking
- Pulling over on the right and reversing
- Driving forwards into a parking bay and reversing back out

So, four manoeuvres for you to learn, but you only do **one** of them on test.

Whatever manoeuvre you're asked to do, they all have three things in common, three things your Examiner will be watching out for:

- Control
- Accuracy
- Observation

Let's start with control…

Try to keep your car moving smoothly and slowly, whatever the gradient. If you're driving a manual transmission car, that means using the clutch with *finesse*, allowing your car to *coast* when appropriate.

The clutch technique used is to lift the clutch slowly to the point where you start to move, keep it still for a couple of seconds, then squeeze it slightly back down again. But just *slightly* back down, not all the way back down – just enough to slow you down until you're almost stopping. Try not to move the clutch, either up or down, abruptly. Try to keep it smooth. Try to creep steadily forward.

Practise first on a level road then add in some gradient, both uphill and downhill.

On a **level** road, try using the clutch without using the accelerator. You'll probably find that at the kinds of speeds you'll be using for manoeuvring it'll work just fine.

When manoeuvring **downhill**, use *controlled coasting.* That's when you press the clutch fully down, simply allowing the car to roll – to *coast* – but then to control the roll with the footbrake, if necessary. Remember: ***Controllin' the rollin'!***

Uphill use *holding point control* – remember, thinking of your clutch as working like a tap – keeping the gas steady at around 2000RPM and controlling the flow of power to the wheels with clutch. Also, remember that a hill start, done in reverse gear, involves lifting the clutch to the point where the bonnet **dips**, instead of rising as would be the case in 1st gear.

Your Examiner also watches your steering…

Dry steering is the name given to turning the steering wheel when the car's stationary. It can cause unnecessary wear-n-tear both to your steering components and to your tyres, so, if possible, try to avoid it. However, if you do need to dry steer – and sometimes it just can't be helped – it isn't marked against you as a fault.

Also, your Examiner's not too concerned about either the position of your hands on the wheel or your steering technique during your manoeuvre. Provided your car's under control, and you're steering accurately, you can pretty much do whatever comes naturally!

So, keep the car under control: move slowly but steer quickly.

Then try to stop smoothly. Nice gentle footbrake, nothing abrupt. And remember that during low speed control it's usually necessary to press the clutch fully down *before* braking.

Finally, when you're changing from first gear into reverse, or vice-versa, keep the car still. Now, that doesn't necessarily mean that you *have* to use your handbrake, but it is probably a good idea, particularly when you're learning a new manoeuvre.

Examiners also want you to manoeuvre accurately...

If you're bay parking, for example, you're expected to finish with all four wheels between the lines. But you don't have to be perfect. Maybe you end up nearer one line than the other, or maybe you end up a bit wonky. No matter. Provided you're in the bay, it's fine.

And you don't necessarily need to get neatly into the parking bay first go. On any manoeuvre, you're allowed to reverse two-or-more times if you need to. So, if you mess up on the reverse part of your manoeuvre, you can always pull forward a couple of metres then reverse back in again.

Also, if you touch a kerb, or go onto a white line, don't panic! Yes, you've made a mistake. Yes, your Examiner has noticed. So, yes, they'll possibly mark your mistake as a fault. But, no, it'll not necessarily be a serious fault. So, no, it'll not necessarily be a fail.

Now, having said that, if you do manage to thump into a kerb or stray miles over a white line, then, yes, unfortunately it might well be scored as a serious fault, so a fail. But, even then, hopefully you'll still be given the benefit of the doubt. And anyway, the last thing you want to do on test is to give up. So if you do touch a kerb or wander over a line try not to worry. Just finish the manoeuvre, finish the test, and keep your fingers crossed!

Finally, your Examiner wants you to be observant...

Very observant. The *observation* aspect of your manoeuvre is the *safety* aspect of your manoeuvre, and the driving test is all about safety.

Before you start your manoeuvre, look around for other traffic and for pedestrians. Check all three mirrors and both blind spots. Wait until everything's clear before you begin.

Then, during the manoeuvre, try to be constantly aware of what's going on around you, including for pedestrians and cyclists.

If other cars turns up, do the opposite to them: if they wait, you can continue; but if they move then you must wait until they've past by.

Before reversing, you MUST look all around, including back between the seats. If you forget, you fail.

Then, as you reverse, look where you're going as much as possible. Look through the back window as well as using your rear-view mirror and side mirrors. Keep checking those blind spots.

If your car has one, you can use a reversing camera, but you must also look around for yourself, not just rely on what's on the screen. Don't just sit there and leave your safety to the tech.

So, during your reversing manoeuvre your Examiner watches your control, accuracy and observation. **But what they _don't_ do is set a stopwatch. Within reason, it doesn't matter how long the manoeuvre takes.** In fact, if you manoeuvre quickly then you're almost certainly not being observant enough to keep your Examiner happy. Take your time. There's no rush.

And, as I'll keep on saying, get loads of practise. Honestly, it's not unusual for learner drivers to need to do each manoeuvre twenty-or-thirty times before they're good at them. And that's with a professional instructor. So, if it's just you and your Supervisor working together then stay super patient with each other!

Anyway, we've talked about manoeuvring in general, so now let's briefly discuss each of the manoeuvres in detail. Remember, though, that on test you're only asked to do one of them.

Let's start with…

Reversing Into A Parking Bay

This is done at the test centre, either at the start or finish of your test, and into a bay either to your left or right. If both sides are available at your Test Centre, you can choose whichever you prefer.

If you're asked to do this at the start of your test, you'll often be required to pull out of the bay you're in and to steer sharply round to get yourself at right angles to the bays, then to straighten up, and then, finally, to go into the reversing part of the manoeuvre. It's tricky.

But if you're doing this at the end of your test, your Examiner will pull you over somewhere in the test centre, then direct you towards the bays.

So, as we said, you can reverse in either to the left or right. Both techniques are essentially the same, so here we'll discuss reversing into a bay that's on your left...

The technique we'll be using only uses the two lines of the actual bay you're reversing into, so isn't affected by bays that have those additional hatched lines surrounding them, and also isn't affected by your bay being the last one in a row.

And this technique also works in a normal sized car park, even with cars parked opposite your bay, because we're not turning away at right-angles from our bay.

So this method of parking will work both on your driving test and also in *real-life* situations.

Start by moving forward, your car perpendicular – at right-angles – to the bay and about a metre away from the end of it, then stop with your shoulder lined-up with the first line of the bay you've chosen – let's call it Line 1.

Line 1 is how you choose the bay you're reversing into.

Line 2 is how you're going to make it happen.

So, Line 2 is the line that's roughly lined up with the front of your car, visible to you somewhere up by your passenger-side door-mirror.

Now, take a moment to look over your left shoulder, through your passenger-side rear-window...

The plan is to get Line 2 to move from its current position, up by the door mirror, all the way back along the car to the back of your passenger-side rear-window.

Let's get to it...

Look all around. If necessary, wait for people to pass by. Then, moving forward slowly, steer one complete turn of the steering-wheel away from the bay (if you'd rather do this first turn while stationary, that's fine), all the while keeping your beady eye on Line 2…

As Line 2 passes your Supervisor's shoulder, take that turn back off, to straighten the steering, with your car now angled slightly away from the bay.

Continue slowly forward until Line 2 reappears in the window *behind* your Supervisor, and watch it continue its journey all the way back to the end of that window. Then stop.

Okay, so that initial turn away from the bay has given you the correct *angle* from the bay, and Line 2 now being at the back of the window behind your Supervisor has given you the correct *distance* from the bay. And if your **angle** and **distance** are spot-on then **full left-lock** will plonk you neatly into the bay, between Lines 1 and 2.

Look all around again. Then reverse, keeping things slow while steering to full left-lock.

Finally, as Line 2 comes into view in your passenger-side door-mirror, begin straightening up.

Once you're in the bay – very important – pause and look all around again…

Check all three mirrors and both blind spots before running back fully into the bay.

Then stop, and finish with handbrake and neutral.

Now, once you're safe-n-sound in the bay, if you want, you can open your door and take a peek at the white line outside, to check your position in the bay. But as long as you're between the lines then that's good enough, even if you're much closer to one line than the other or you're a bit wonky.

So, it's only if you're on or over a line that you'll need to pull forward a bit, steering as necessary to get yourself between the lines, and reverse back in again.

Stay slow, stay observant – especially for pedestrians – and take your time.

Next, it's...

Parallel Parking

Your Examiner asks you to pull over at the side of the road, then points to a car parked in front of you and says something like, *I'd like you to pull up alongside the car in front of us. Then use reverse gear to park close-to-and-parallel-with the kerb, stopping roughly within two car lengths of the car.*

But before we discuss this manoeuvre...

Note: try not to get this exercise confused with the **angled start** that we introduced in Lesson 6 then revised in Lesson 15. It's not unknown for folk who have been asked to **pull over close to the vehicle up-ahead** (to do an angled start) to think their Examiner wants them to pull up **alongside** that car and then go straight into a **parallel park...**

Remember, being asked to pull over *close* to a car means you're being asked to position yourself for an *angled start* NOT a *parallel park.*

Okay, so let's start this manoeuvre by taking a quick look into your passenger-side door-mirror... You can see your car in there, and you can see the kerb, running parallel with your car. Now, in a few moments time – when you're reversing in towards the kerb – in your mirror you'll still be able to see your car, same as you do now, but the kerb will no longer be parallel, instead, it'll be at a forty-five degree angle to your car...

So, from your start position, make sure you're clear all around –

nothing coming from front or back – and pull out from the kerb to move up alongside the car ahead. You're aiming to be about a metre away from it, parallel with it, with your wheels straight. If the other car is pointing in the same direction as you, aim to line up your door mirror with theirs.

When you stop, indicate left, keep your footbrake on and select reverse gear. So, you've now got your indicator flashing, your brake lights on and your white reversing light on. The back of your car's lit up like a Christmas tree!

Look all around again. Wait for any passing traffic and for pedestrians crossing behind you or walking close to you on the footpath. All clear? Okay, you're ready to start reversing…

Reverse slowly, steering three-quarters of a turn of the steering-wheel towards the kerb. After about a car length, when you're pointing diagonally across the road, aiming at the kerb, angled in at about forty-five degrees, straighten-up…

Now, keep the car still and look all around. Be especially careful of cars approaching from behind, as they'll be in your blind spot, over your right shoulder.

Now reverse another car length-or-so to your reference point…

Remember your reference point here will be in your passenger-side door-mirror…

As you approach the kerb, you'll see a *tarmac* triangle in the mirror, made up of your car's bodywork, the kerb, and the bottom of the mirror. As you reverse, watch how this triangle – so the amount of tarmac you can see – shrinks. Then, when the triangle's tiny, stop.

By stopping at this reference point – the triangle – two things happen. First: stopping will always be more accurate than trying to find your reference point on the move.

And, second: by stopping, you ensure that you have plenty of time to look all around, so you won't need to rush your all-important all-round observation.

All clear? Okay, so moving slowly again, steer round quickly to **full right-lock**. At this point, your car's virtually pivoting around on your driver's-side rear-wheel, swinging into the parking space. And let it swing in, until you're parallel with the kerb, then stop.

So, how far are you from the kerb? Miles away? Next time, get a little closer and use a slightly smaller triangle. Touching the kerb? Next time, stop a little earlier, so you can see a bit more tarmac in the mirror – a larger triangle – before steering in.

Try this *tarmac triangle* technique a couple of times. It won't be long before you'll be able to consistently find an accurate reference point and have the car swinging into the kerb perfectly!

Finally, as you do swing into the kerb, try to find time to take some of the steering back off – perhaps just half-a-turn – just before parallel, so just before you stop, to neaten things up slightly.

Though, remember, your Examiner asked you to finish *close to, and parallel with, the kerb*, but they didn't say that you must have the wheels completely straight. So, if you don't find time to take any steering off, don't worry. The important thing is to finish parallel with the kerb, whichever way your wheels are pointing!

So, when you're parallel with the kerb, you're finished.

Secure the car: handbrake and neutral.

You're done.

Next...

Pulling Over On The Right Then Reversing For Two Car Lengths

So, there you are, on test, driving down a street, when your Examiner asks you to, *pull over on the right-hand side of the road, when it's safe to do so.*

Back to basics. Don't park blocking bus-stops or driveways, don't stop close to junctions, including opposite them. And don't stop close to a parked car – it's only going to make it tricky to see past it, in a minute-or-two, when you're asked to move away again.

Anyway, choose your spot then prepare as if to turn right. So, mirrors, indicators, position in the road, then give way to oncoming traffic before moving across to the right-hand kerb.

Line the kerb up in your windscreen, maybe six inches-or-so in from the right-hand edge of it, then straighten your steering, stop, and secure the car.

Now your Examiner says, *reverse for about two car lengths, keeping reasonably close to the kerb.*

Into reverse, look all around, including forwards, then reverse slowly. You're trying to stay parallel with the kerb, around a foot-or-so – so thirty centimetres – from it. You can use the door mirror to help you gauge your distance from the kerb, but try to look back, through the rear window, as much as possible.

Find a point on the lower edge of your back window where the kerb lines up, then, if you need to adjust your steering, only use small amounts, no more than a quarter turn of the wheel at a time, and remember that, if things go pear-shaped, you can always pull forward a touch, straighten up, and reverse again.

Now, if you find it tricky to reverse in a straight line, it could be because you're thinking in terms of turning right or left. So, instead, think of turning the wheel either **towards** or **away** from the kerb – towards and away from the kerb are the same whether you're driving forwards or backwards.

Throughout this straight reverse, try to keep your observation going. Look back, to watch for pedestrians and guys driving out of their driveways, and also look forwards, stopping if any oncoming traffic passes by.

After a couple of car lengths, stop again and secure the car. As usual, try not to block any driveways or bus-stops.

Finally, your Examiner will simply ask you to, **move away when you're ready**.

This is tricky because you have to give-way to oncoming traffic as well as those coming up behind you, and you're going to have to drive all the way across from the right-hand side, back over to the left-hand side, of the road. So you'll need nice big gaps in traffic from both directions before you indicate left, check the left blind-spot – one last time – and move away.

Oh, and if during the time it takes you to do this manoeuvre another car turns up and parks in front of you, making it really difficult for you to take safe observation before moving away, then your Examiner will hopefully step in to assist you, giving you updates on any oncoming traffic.

Okay! Nearly there. The last one is…

Driving Forwards Into A Parking Bay Then Reversing Back Out

…and it's done in a local car park. So, as you enter the car park, watch for direction signs and arrows, speed limit signs and, of course, pedestrians.

Your Examiner will ask you to select a bay – it could be on your right or left – and to drive forwards into it and park.

Use your mirrors, indicate, and check your blind-spot before you start your turn into the bay.

Your reference point for steering-in will be in the respective side window of the side you're driving into. Again, practise to find a couple of spots in the side windows – left and right – that work for you. The idea is to reach your reference point, then to steer in with full-lock, straightening up as you enter the bay.

Like the other manoeuvres, if you don't manage to steer accurately into the bay on the first attempt, you can reverse back out a car length-or-so, and try again.

Anyway, once you're in the bay, with the car secure, your Examiner will ask you to reverse back out of the space and drive away.

If the car park has a one-way system, think which way you'll need to reverse in order to be facing in the right direction – which will probably be back out the way you came in!

Now, as you reverse, the danger here is in the front of your car swinging round and potentially scraping against any cars parked alongside you, if you steer too soon…

So, as you reverse, stay perfectly straight for around three-quarters of the length of your car, before steering round, all the while being aware of what the front of your car's doing.

Also, safe observation when reversing out of a parking bay can be really tricky. That's why, given half-a-chance, rather than drive in, it's better to reverse into spaces and then drive out. Anyway, take your time and wait for any passing traffic or pedestrians.

*

Okay, you've now got your general driving up to speed and you're all set to tackle your emergency stop and reversing manoeuvre, so let's talk about…

WHAT TO EXPECT
ON TEST DAY

Lesson 18

As we said at the beginning of this book, lots of folk, after failing a driving test, will say, *oh well, at least I know what to expect next time.* But, with preparation, even a first driving test needn't catch you out with any nasty surprises.

When it comes to your driving test, it's simple: the better you are at driving, the higher your chance of success. But knowing what to expect on test day is also important. So, in this lesson, we're again going to be looking at preparation for the test, but preparation that goes **beyond** the actual driving.

So, first, we'll look at the importance of visiting your local test centre, getting a feel for both the place and for what goes on there. Then we'll run through:

- Test nerves
- Booking your test
- In the test centre
- Your car
- The eyesight test
- Your Examiner
- Terminated tests
- Minor traffic accidents
- The result

But, before we crack on with those, let's have a quick word about the importance of visiting the test centre beforehand…

The centre you'll be using might not exactly be what you'd call *local*. It might be miles away. But gaining the experience of driving in there and parking, of walking over to the waiting area, of watching someone on *their* test – a test **candidate** – heading over to their car with their Examiner, watching them doing their eyesight test and safety question, then watching them driving away… All that stuff's pure gold when it comes to your test preparation.

You can check driving test start times online, so as to time your visit to the test centre to watch an actual test getting underway. Then, when that test has gone, take a look at the layout of the road system there, the speed limit and the direction arrows.

Also check-out the parking bays used by test candidates before and after the test. Sometimes you might start your test from a designated *Driving Test* bay but then finish in a public area of the test centre's car park. And sometimes tests might even start or finish outside the actual test centre, on the public road.

Then get a feel for the roads and junctions around the test centre. Look at the area on a map. How many ways in and out of the immediate area are there? Chances are, driving test routes will take in all of those roads and junctions, so spend some time getting to know your way around.

You should be able to visualise the junctions around the test centre – be able to draw a diagram of them – the lanes, the directions to local towns, so that if your Examiner says, *head towards London* you'll know what that means.

Now, I'm not suggesting that in order to pass a test you need a detailed knowledge of all the routes, but there's no doubt that a familiarity with the roads surrounding the test centre will help massively.

Okay, so back to our list for this lesson. Let's talk about…

Driving Test Nerves

Everybody gets nervous. But what are you getting nervous about? As we said at the beginning of this lesson, often folk get nervous over the idea that they don't know what to expect. That's where this book comes in!

So break the test down in your mind. Visualise it. Folk say they're nervous but can't pin-point what they're nervous of.

What about you? Are you nervous of any particular aspect of the test? A particular junction or manoeuvre? If so, try to find time to deal with those concerns, to clear them up.

Are you nervous about getting a particular Examiner? If so, remember that, at the end of the day, even though some are said to be *nicer* than others, they all have the same pass rate.

Are you nervous about the way you think you might react to the pressure of the test? Again, visualisation will help, imagining yourself doing well – handling a particularly tricky local junction well – and imagining yourself being photographed by your Supervisor, a big test-pass smile on your face!

Also, remember that most people, however nervous they are beforehand, are fine once their test begins. The nerves you're feeling are **pre-test**.

Are you possibly even nervous about the idea that **after** the test, when you pass, you'll be expected to drive on your own? If so, either book an extra lesson with your Instructor for the day after the test, or else raise those concerns with your Supervisor, to make sure you won't simply be thrown to the wolves from Day 1, nervously clutching your 'P' plate!

Try to think positively about the benefits driving will bring.

Think of yourself driving along on sunny days to meet up with friends, then think of all those dreary waits at the bus stop you'll be waving goodbye to!

Driving is brilliant! And on that note, let's talk about…

Booking Your Test

You can only book a practical test if you've passed the theory test within the past two years.

Now, be honest with yourself. Do you really want to book *that* test for next Tuesday just because it's the first one available? Yes, you can **book** a test, by all means, but don't expect to **pass** a test unless you can drive safely, without any more than the occasional word of advice from your Supervisor. If you're still being reminded to change gear or to brake, or who has priority at junctions, then you need a lot more driving experience.

There's no secret here: the more you drive the better you get. So practise as much as you can and continue to revise. Oh, and also re-read *The Highway Code*. Those things that you once only thought of as *theory* will make much more sense now that you're thinking of your *practical* driving test. Your theory was like reading the rules of a sport you've never played. Now you're in the game.

Book the test online, at the official – GOV.UK – website. The official website doesn't charge a booking fee. The rip-off sites do. Book a test date that gives you plenty of time for the all-important mock tests and final revision.

And book your test for a sensible time. Late morning, perhaps. I mean, do you really want to be adding to the stress of doing a driving test by doing it in the middle of the school run? Hopefully you'll only ever take one driving test in your lifetime, so why worry if you have to wait another week-or-two for a good time to do it?

Anyway, now that you've taken a drive up to your local test centre, and you've also got a test booked, let's talk about what happens on test day...

In The Test Centre

Well, on the day, don't be late! But don't be too early, either. About ten minutes before your test appointment is perfect. Not half-an-hour, you'll just be sitting there, getting more-n-more nervous!

Find yourself one of the designated parking spaces for driving test candidates. Now, at the start of your test, the last thing you want is to have to reverse *out* of the space. So reverse in, if necessary, so that you can simply drive away forwards.

Then grab your paperwork, car keys, and glasses if you use them, and head over to the waiting room...

In the waiting room you usually don't need to report to anyone that you've arrived, so just take a seat, then at the appointed time your Examiner will come to find you. But some test centres might have a little buzzer, or whatever, to press.

Then get your paperwork ready for your Examiner to...er... *examine*. They'll want to see your provisional licence and your theory test pass letter. And also your passport, if your licence **doesn't** include photographic ID.

However, if you can't find any of your documents, I know it's worrying, but remember that if you didn't have a valid licence or if you hadn't passed a theory test then the DVSA's computer simply wouldn't even have allowed you to book a practical driving test. So, even if you haven't been able to find any of your driving documentation, provided you turn up at the test centre with a *valid* photo ID, your test should still go ahead.

Having said that, if you're still unsure about your documentation, either ring DVSA or your local test centre for advice.

Okay, so as we said, when you finally meet your Examiner, they'll check your driving documents. They'll also ask you to sign a declaration to confirm that your car's legal for you to drive on the test, and for you to check the email address they have on record for you, for your pass confirmation to be sent to.

Then they'll ask you if you'd like your Supervisor to accompany you out on the test, so for them to sit in the back of the car.

Discuss with your Supervisor beforehand what your answer's going to be.

The advantage of someone going with you is that, especially if you fail, your Supervisor will have seen first-hand the mistakes you made. The disadvantage is that you might feel under even more pressure, what with two people watching your every move! It's up to you.

Anyway, formalities completed, Examiner smiling, butterflies turning somersaults in your stomach, you finally head out to the car park to start the test. Now, on test, for the price of your fee, the DVSA has supplied you with a Driving Examiner but not with a car. Small detail, I know, but you have to supply one of those yourself!

So let's make sure you're organised, let's sort out…

Your Car

Though, hopefully, it'll be your Supervisor who'll take care of that for you! Anyway, just in case…

Well, it needs to be legal, obviously. Taxed, insured, valid MOT. And, if you have them, you might as well take all the documents with you, in case there's a problem with anything.

And your car needs to be roadworthy. Just waving an MOT certificate around won't impress anyone if your exhaust's clearly hanging off. And your car needs four good tyres. And head restraints. And 'L' plates – set so that they don't block the Examiner's view. And, yes, they will check all this stuff.

Same goes for the lights. If your Examiner notices that one's not working, your test might not go ahead. Warning lights, too. If the dashboard's telling them – via the **engine management** warning light – that the car has a problem, then they won't take you out on test.

You also need a mirror, fixed to the windscreen, for your Examiner's use. One of those suction-cup ones is perfect. They cost a tenner.

Finally, give your pride-n-joy a clean. Clean cars drive better, everyone knows that! And a freshly washed-n-vacuumed car, with nice clean windows, will give your Examiner a positive impression of you and your preparation.

Now, if there is a problem with your car and, for whatever reason, your Examiner refuses to take you out on test, I'm afraid you'll lose your fee and you'll have to re-book. So make sure you've done your homework and everything's sorted.

In the test centre, as we've discussed, hopefully you've parked neatly in a parking space, ideally one reserved for driving test candidates, one that's easy for you to drive away from. So, remember, if necessary, reverse in.

Finally, remember that your test will usually be at the same time as other test candidates, so the centre could be busy with those other folk arriving at the same time as you. Also, try not to get in the way of guys returning from tests. There's often only a few minutes between one test finishing and another starting, so keep out of the way, especially of cars doing reverse parking manoeuvres.

Okay, now things are getting serious. Picture yourself heading over to your car with your Examiner... When, suddenly, your Examiner stops, asks you to stand next to them, and tells you that you're going to start with an...

Eyesight Test

You're asked to read a parked car's number-plate from twenty-odd metres away...

No problem? Great. Yes problem?

Well...now your Examiner heads back into the test centre for a tape measure. Yes...seriously. Then they measure an exact twenty metres away from another parked car and get you to try again. And if you still can't read it then I'm afraid you've just failed your driving test.

On the plus side, though, you have had a *free* eye test!

But that's not all. If you fail your driving test in this way then your licence is **revoked** – torn up – and you'll have to apply for another provisional licence, except this time you'll have to do an actual eyesight test **before** you're given that new licence.

So make sure your eyesight is up to scratch *before* test day!

Oh, and yes, if you wear contacts or glasses then you can do the eyesight test with those in-or-on, but then you must do the rest of the test with them, too.

Now, I know we've already discussed your Examiner in Lesson 15, but this lesson still wouldn't be complete without another quick word on...

Your Driving Examiner

Their work schedule for the day allows them around fifty minutes for each test candidate. But that includes the five minutes the two of you have already spent together – meeting in the test centre and now out in the car park.

Then you'll spend around thirty-five minutes out on the actual drive, then another five minutes-or-so back in the car park, after the drive, where your Examiner will discuss your test drive with you before they, hopefully, organise your shiny new driving licence.

After that, they wish you well, dash back to their office – super quick – for a coffee, before then heading back round to the waiting room for their next victim. Sorry, not victim, **test candidate…**

So, after all your hours-upon-hours of preparation, and your miles-upon-miles of driving, it all comes down to these next thirty-five minutes.

Every one of those miles, and every one of those hours, are like cash in a savings account – they all add up – and now you're going to make the big withdrawal, you're going to put everything you've saved into passing this test.

Now, everybody who is thoroughly prepared – and I mean everybody – tells me afterwards that their test flew by. In fact, strange as it may sound to you now, many folk tell me they actually *enjoyed* their driving test…

It's that feeling: the day is finally here, so pre-test nerves are fading, adrenaline is kicking in… You're confident as a driver, you've practised your manoeuvres until you're doing them in your sleep, you're familiar with your car and your surroundings, you've realised that your Examiner's actually a really nice person, and it's slowly dawning on you that you're going to get through this, that you might actually pass this thing.

But if, on the other hand, you're not prepared for this, it could turn into a very long half-an-hour indeed. Because, although, yes, your Examiner is a really nice person, they're not one of your friends, so they're not here to help you out.

In fact, in some cases, you could even suffer from...

A Terminated Test!

So, in a really extreme situation, either you or your Examiner might decide to call it a day, to call the test off, part-way through: to *terminate* it.

It's rare but it can happen.

Maybe your brain has just gone into meltdown and you've jumped a red light. You've never done it before, but *hey*, these things happen. So you tell your Examiner that you're aware of your mistake and that you no longer wish to continue with the test.

Your Examiner replies that it's up to you, that they completely understand. Then they direct you to pull over to the side of the road. Once you're safe and secure, they ask you to turn off the engine. They'll talk to you briefly about the drive, hopefully even giving you a couple of positives to take away from the experience...

But then they get out of the car and leave you!

Yep. Leave you! You are abandoned! So, no, they don't drive you back to the test centre. Wherever you end up stopping, that's where you're left. OMG! So then you'd need to phone your Supervisor to have them come out to collect both you and the car. And that could take ages.

So – unless it's a really extreme situation – **don't give up**.

Folk who give up are left demoralised and deflated. They might even question whether this driving lark is really for them. But, on the other hand, if, after making a horrendous mistake, you just pull on your big-boy (or girl) pants and finish the test then you'll gain the experience of having driven a proper driving test route with a proper Driving Examiner, who will have given you proper feedback on your drive. So, even though you failed, you got your money's worth and, more importantly, your confidence will have survived the ordeal.

Reaching the point where you can drive around a test route with an Examiner is a huge step along the way to becoming a good driver. But not everyone passes first time. Some need two-or-three goes. But it's not the end of the world if you don't pass first time. Everyone gets there eventually. And the experience and the confidence you'll gain from completing a test – even if you don't pass – means you'll be right back in there, even more determined to pass next time.

So, please, don't give up.

And that includes if you're involved in a…

Minor Traffic Accident

Picture it, there you are, waiting at a roundabout, searching for a gap, when…BANG. You've been rear-ended. Nightmare. But, try not to panic. Breathe.

Then get out. Take photos. Take a name, a registration number, an address and a phone number. Take a note of any damage. But don't expect any help from your Examiner. Your test isn't over (unless you tell your Examiner that you wish to *terminate* it!). *This* is now part of your test! Dealing with this situation is still all down to you.

All sorted? So, how are you feeling? How's your Examiner feeling? How's your car feeling? Lights still working? Well, if everyone and everything's okay, and you've got enough detail to accurately report the crash to your insurance company, you can leave the scene of the bump and continue with your test. After all, you didn't do anything wrong, so you haven't failed.

But nobody in this situation would blame you for giving up. I certainly wouldn't. But maybe – *hopefully* – you're made of stronger stuff. Maybe you're determined to see it through. I hope so.

Okay, so over the course of your driving test you'll do:

- An eyesight test
- A stationary *tell me* safety question
- A driving *show me* safety question
- Around twenty minutes of independent driving
- A reversing manoeuvre
- A hill start
- An angled start
- An emergency stop

Your Examiner might not get you to do everything on that list, but it's best to be prepared, just in case they do. But, whatever you're asked to do, soon enough you'll be back at the test centre, car parked, engine off, and your Examiner will turn to you and deliver…

The Result

You've passed! Your Examiner gives you a quick run-down on where you could improve your driving then asks for your licence so that they can arrange for your **full** licence to be posted out to you. Now, if for some reason you'd prefer to hold on to your provisional licence for a while, that's fine. But then you've got just **two years** to update it yourself…

Two years? That's ages! But is it really? You definitely don't want to join the list of folk who've messed up and forgotten. They've had to re-sit both the theory and practical tests – had to do the lot – all over again.

So, unless you have a really good reason not to, give your Examiner your provisional licence!

And now you can drive anywhere. You can drive on the motorway. You can drive at night, drive in the rain, take passengers…the world is your oyster.

Today is now the first day of your two year *probation period*. Two years. If you get **six penalty points** within those two years then your licence is *revoked*. Remember, that means torn up. Revoked doesn't mean you're banned, though. So, theoretically, you could still drive…just as soon as you've done your theory test and driving test all over again, that is! Yep, you have to start over from scratch.

And six points isn't six offences. Speeding offences aren't just one point each. Most offences carry a three-point penalty. Some will even get you all six points in one go.

Don't panic, though, there isn't a police constable waiting for you on every street corner. But, if you do start to take silly risks, well, there's a fair chance you'll be joining those hundreds of new drivers who, every year, have their licences revoked.

Oh, and of course, it's not a bad idea to replace your old 'L' plates with a fresh set of 'P' plates. It's not mandatory but it's worth considering. We all make mistakes and especially during those first few weeks it could be a literal life-saver if the traffic around knows you're a newly qualified driver and so is half-expecting you to make a mistake! So bang a couple on your motor, *just in case!*

So that's if you pass. But what if you fail? Well, first of all, commiserations. But don't be put off. Listen carefully to your Examiner's feedback, then apply for another test, get lots more driving practise, and pass next time!

And on that cheerful note, let's get you super-ready for that test of yours. Let's talk about...

MOCK TESTS

Lesson 19

Mock testing is to get you used to driving for extended periods of time without instruction.

Note, though, that **without instruction** doesn't mean driving without being given **directions**. No, it means being left on your own to choose gears, speeds, lanes…forcing you to work on your **decision making**.

Yes, your Supervisor is there with you, but only to direct you around the route and to help keep you safe in the event of a potentially dangerous situation. They're not there to instruct you. So, if you need instruction, or if you find yourself asking for help, then that test is a *fail*.

If you've never had the experience of driving **on your own** for half-an-hour-or-so then you're less likely to pass a driving test than a learner driver who has. To pass a test, you don't need to be perfect but you *do* need to be able to drive on your own.

It's not uncommon for instructors to have pupils who seem to be coming along nicely – good car control, good understanding of the road – but pupils who, at every roundabout, will quietly ask, *can I go now?*

It's the ability to make those *can I go now* decisions that's the final piece of the puzzle.

Another reason for mock testing is for you to be presented – in stark black-n-white – with the mistakes you made over the entire drive…

Up to now, your Supervisor has probably been correcting most of your mistakes on the go, one at a time. But sometimes those mistakes will be glossed-over, either because there just isn't the possibility to discuss them at the time, or else because something seemingly more important crops up. Either way, they might not always be sufficiently rectified.

But after a mock test you're being told – cold as ice – that you would have failed your test for this, this and this! And, chances are, many of those mistake you would've just classed as *silly* mistakes. Well, call them whatever you like, and I appreciate it can be hard to hear, but they were real mistakes – silly or not – and it's definitely better to hear about them now, rather than at the end of a real test.

Let's get to it.

Start with a mix of about a dozen junctions, something that'll take ten minutes to drive around, in an area that you know reasonably well. Do the first lap as normal, your Supervisor offering advice and instruction on the go. Then do another lap, this time with your Supervisor merely directing you: **at the end of the road, turn left** – that kind of thing. Stop and start a few times. As you do this lap, your Supervisor takes notes.

Here, amongst other things, we're looking at your:

- Use of mirrors and blind spot checks
- Car control
- Timing of signals
- Road positioning
- Approach speeds
- Choice of gears
- Giving way where necessary
- Acceleration and use of speed
- Decision making

Your Supervisor starts with a blank sheet of paper and makes a quick note of any mistakes they see. Then, afterwards, the two of you talk through those mistakes, before you head out onto lap three, correcting the mistakes as you go.

Then, finally, it's Lap 4. On your own again, this time hopefully not making the same mistakes as on Lap 2, but quite possibly making a couple of new ones! That's okay. That's normal.

Try doing a few of these fairly easy routes. Then move on to tackling routes that take-in a few more complex junctions – a couple of roundabouts and a few sets of traffic lights – routes that take fifteen-to-twenty minutes, and follow the same procedure:

- Warm up lap
- Mock test
- Correction lap
- Second mock test

Also try doing a few routes following directions from a sat-nav. The one on your phone's fine. Pick a destination that's roughly twenty minutes away, set the machine up, and let it lead the way...

It'll get you used to following monotone, dull, dry directions – so perfect practise for when you meet your Examiner! – and it's also good practise for the *independent driving* that you might be asked to do on your test.

Next, try the same thing with your manoeuvres. Do a couple with supervision, to warm up, then tackle one on your own, start-to-finish.

Remember, the key to passing a driving test is to be able to drive unaided. If you still need help from your Supervisor then you'll definitely get found out by your Examiner.

Finally, when you've built up to doing each of these exercises a few times, it's time to move onto a full mock test.

Work-out a route that takes in a mix of roads and junction types, that has suitable places for a hill start, angled start, emergency stop, and a reverse manoeuvre, a route that'll take a full thirty minutes to drive round. Try to take this seriously. No chatting. During the drive, ask your Supervisor to clarify any instruction you don't understand. Focus on your driving.

Now, on the drive, you're going to make mistakes. But don't give up. Sort yourself out and carry on. Get around the route. Get it done.

And don't be disheartened. Very few people pass a first or second mock test. Remember, your goal is to drive the route unaided, or at least *virtually* unaided, then to get any mistakes you've made presented to you to reflect on and work on.

Like doing theory practise tests on your App, when you're passing practical mock tests comfortably then you know you'll pass a real driving test easily, too.

Which will set you up nicely for...

TEST DAY

Lesson 20

Like most exams, your driving test prep starts the day before. So, if you're using your own car, give it a quick wash-n-vacuum and clean the windows. Check the tyres, check the lights, and make sure it has plenty of fuel. Oh, and remember to get a stick-on rear-view mirror for your Examiner to use.

Get your car's paperwork together, stick it in a nice big envelope, and put it somewhere that will remind you to take it with you in the morning. Then find both parts of your driving licence and your theory-test pass-letter, and stick those in the nice big envelope, too.

Do you wear glasses? Find them, give them a clean, and put them with your nice big envelope. Organise your contacts, if you use those. Oh, and grab your sunglasses. Yes, of course you can wear them if it's sunny.

Then add a small bottle of water and a snack, in case you get thirsty or peckish.

Oh, and you'd be amazed how many people turn up for their test on the wrong date or at the wrong time. So check those now. Then check that your Supervisor is also organised for the big day.

Then do some revision. Out in your car, if possible, but if not…

Remember all that stuff that you called *theory*? Well tomorrow it changes from theory to **real**. Do you remember the rules for pedestrian crossings? Zigzag lines and flashing amber lights? What about if a traffic light's not working? Visualise you driving, and the difference between a give-way line and a stop line.

Take some time to revise *The Highway Code*.

And give some thought to what you're going to wear tomorrow. Something comfy but not too warm. Something that makes you feel good without making you look like you're going to a wedding. Sensible shoes.

Finally, plan for an early night, phone on charge but set to silent, and set your alarm.

So, to recap, the day before…

- Double-check you've got the right time and date
- Confirm times with your Supervisor
- Find both parts of your driving licence and theory test letter
- Find any documents you might need for your car
- Water and snack
- Glasses, contacts or sunglasses
- Clean your car
- Mirror for your Examiner
- Check the tyres and lights
- Fuel
- Revise
- Clothes
- Charge your phone
- Set your alarm

On the day, give yourself plenty of time for the drive over to the test centre. You want enough time for a couple of practise manoeuvres on the way over, to get yourself up-to-speed.

Some people are absolutely fine on the drive over to the test centre, others…well…not so much! You may find you make lots of mistakes! But don't panic. That's pre-test nerves messing with your head. Some people drive really slowly on the way over, some go at it like a rally driver. Again, don't panic – this is all normal.

Remember, these are pre-test nerves. Like a school exam. When you turn over that exam paper and write your name, the nerves fade. And here, as you drive your Examiner away from the test centre, you'll be fine as well.

If you've been to the test centre before, arrive there around ten-to-fifteen minutes before your test appointment. But, if you've never had chance to visit and look around, allow yourself five minutes longer, to give yourself time to get a feel for the place.

Try not to get in the way of guys coming into the test centre at the end of their tests. So watch for 'L' drivers, especially those with passengers wearing fluorescent jackets.

Also remember to park your car so that you can drive forwards, away from the space you've chosen. Have a chat with your Supervisor about possible manoeuvres you might be asked to do at the test centre. Talk about your likely routes away from the centre, and also any possible routes you might use on the way back in. Try to picture the actual junctions and the lanes you'd use.

Then grab your stuff – including your glasses, if you wear them – and head over to the waiting room.

Find a seat and wait. Unless there's a sign telling you otherwise, your Examiner will come to you. Double-check that you have your paperwork, glasses and also your car keys.

Five minutes to go. Take a drink of water. Use the bathroom. Have your licence and theory pass letter ready for your Examiner.

Then your Examiner appears. There are smiles and

introductions. They check your documents and ask you to sign to confirm that your car's legal. They ask if you want your Supervisor to accompany you on test.

Then they lead you outside, and over to the car park, where you'll do your eyesight test, before finally heading over to your nice clean car.

Arriving at the car, you're asked your *tell me* safety question. Then you'll be invited to make yourself comfortable in the driver's seat, while your Examiner gives the car a quick once-over.

Now you're in, sitting comfortably – so no coats or scarves – seatbelt on. Then your Examiner climbs into the passenger seat. They adjust their mirror, the one stuck to the windscreen for them.

Then, at long last, your Examiner starts the driving part of the test. They say something like: *I'd like you to follow the road ahead unless signs or road markings indicate otherwise. If I want you to turn, I'll tell you in good time. Move on when you're ready, please.*

Okay, this is it. Control your breathing. Make sure the car's *secure* then start the engine. Into gear. Have a good look around. Are any other driving test candidates moving away at exactly the same time as you? If so, watch them carefully, they might be even more nervous than you!

Finally, after all the weeks and months of practise, you're off. Remember, this test will fly by. You'll be on your way back in no time. Try to do the basics well: mirrors, blind spot checks, moving away procedure...

Drive carefully, keeping things as smooth as possible. You want your Examiner to feel comfortable and relaxed. At junctions, allow yourself plenty of time, no sudden movements. Drive like a chauffeur, not like you're late for work. Remember, your Examiner will be quick to fail you if you're too quick, but slow to fail you if you're too slow. So take your time. There's no rush.

On the drive you'll be doing:

- An independent drive
- A reversing manoeuvre
- A hill start
- An angled start
- An emergency stop
- Your *show me* safety question

Anyway, in no time at all you'll be on your way back to the test centre, possibly even recognising the route home. Then you'll be back at the test centre, engine off, awaiting the moment of truth…

The result…

Good luck!

(You're gonna need it!)

Just kiddin'!

*

Thank you for taking the time to read this book. I hope you go on to enjoy a lifetime of safe – but occasionally adventurous – driving.

Finally, if you've enjoyed this book, please give it a good review on Amazon and on your social media. Good reviews are the lifeblood of independent authors.

Have fun but stay safe out on the road.

Peace

Mark